Bald

Bald

35 Philosophical Short Cuts

SIMON CRITCHLEY

Essays Edited by Peter Catapano

Yale UNIVERSITY PRESS

New Haven and London

Yale University Press books may be purchased in quantity for educational, business, or promotional use. For information, please e-mail sales.press@yale.edu (U.S. office) or sales@yaleup.co.uk (U.K. office).

Set in Minion type by IDS Infotech, Ltd.
Printed in the United States of America.

Library of Congress Control Number: 2020946698
ISBN 978-0-300-25596-6 (hardcover : alk. paper)

A catalogue record for this book is available from the British Library.

This paper meets the requirements of ANSI/NISO Z39.48-1992 (Permanence of Paper).

10 9 8 7 6 5 4 3 2 1

The Material was originally published in *The New York Times*.

Contents

Others

Philip K. Dick, Garage Philosopher

Covid Coda

Preface

I'm bald. Aged around nineteen, I noticed that my frontal hair-line had begun to recede on the sides, ever so subtly, and narrow into the clear V-shape of a widow's peak. I made light of the fact with friends, safe in the knowledge that my father (who, according to my Uncle Ray, had an unusual terror of baldness) had the same hairline but had retained a thick head of dark hair until his death.

Later, around twenty-two or twenty-three, I kept finding hair on my pillow in the morning or clogged around the plughole in the bath. Rigging up an improvised apparatus, I tried to get a proper look at the back of my head. With the aid of an Angle-poise lamp on a desk and by kneeling in an attitude of prayer in front of a dressing mirror with a small shaving mirror in the palm of my right hand high above my head, I saw, indisputably, that the hair on the crown of my head was thinning, with patches of scalp visible through the brown wisps. I don't remember quite what I felt at the time, but it surely was not joy.

From then on—like the Roman Empire—my hair went into a long and irreversible decline and fall. Like many men, I tried a variety of increasingly desperate makeshift hairstyles, growing it, cutting it, parting it, shaping it this way and that, even using hair gel to generate the illusion of volume and luster (but never fully resorting to the dreaded comb-over). Around forty, in a barber shop in Sydney, I finally had it all shaved off and have remained a baldy ever since.

I heard that baldness depended on one's maternal grand-father. Mine had died relatively young, when I was about eight years old, so I studied black-and-white photos taken in Liverpool in the 1940s and 1950s. But my grandad, Tom Pearce, had a fine head of hair and an unusually low hairline above his unsmiling face (bad teeth). Since my other grandfather's hair looked like an old-fashioned thickly bristled doormat, I was perplexed.

My mother and my sister were both hairdressers and liked to experiment on me. Was this my revenge against them? I asked myself. My mother never forgave me for going bald. She was fond of declaring, often to no one in particular, "Si, you used to have such lovely hair! Why did you lose it?" I often wondered whether I had somehow conspired in my hairlessness.

The funny thing about being bald is that it's perfectly all right for people, even in polite society, to point out the fact: "Hey, baldy!" Why is it considered acceptable to point out that men are involuntarily tonsured? I mean, it's not all right to call some-one "fatty" or "shorty," but why are either explicit or surreptitious allusions to one's lack of hair considered an acceptable currency of social exchange? The happily hirsute world would be surprised how often this happens, often in sneaky and snide little quips.

In the Second Book of Kings, the bald biblical prophet Elisha was ridiculed by youths as he made his way to Bethel. "Go up, you baldhead!," they shouted, or "Stye up, ballard," as John Wycliffe's fourteenth-century translation nicely puts it (the surname Ballard probably means "bald head"). After Elisha had cursed them, two female bears came out of the woods and mauled forty-two of the youths, which is quite a lot of youths.

Admittedly, this is going a little far. Female bears can be hard to find and no doubt harder to train. To be clear, I don't want to claim baldness as some kind of identity in a sport of competitive victimization, nor do I want to address some silent confederacy of the hairless and stir them up into a new political movement of the bald: "Rise up, Ballards!"

No, it's a different sense of baldness that I want to draw attention to in framing the thirty-five essays in this book, written over the past decade or so for *The New York Times*. Let me explain with a joke. My father had three favorite gags. One involved Jesus on the cross and another was about a flatulent ballerina. His second-best joke was the following:

> I never left the house as a child. My family were so poor that my mother couldn't afford to buy us clothes. When I was ten, my mother bought me a hat so that I could look out the window.

Maybe this is not the funniest joke in the world, but he used to fall about laughing after telling it, and so did I. He must have told it to me at least once a year.

The baldness that I want to emphasize here consists in not waiting for your mother to buy you a hat but sticking your head out of the window nonetheless. The essays collected here are my attempt to stick my bald head out of the window and think in public.

There are two main senses of the word "bald": hairless and blunt, in the sense of a bald statement or speaking in a plain, unadorned, unveiled and indeed slightly stark way. As an academic, one gets used to speaking with a lot of protective headgear, which one can arrange into an elaborate scholastic toupee. Language can easily become covert, full of hesitations, clever qualifications, impersonal phrasing, passive voice constructions, subordinate clauses, intimidating polysyllabic jargon, name-dropping and arguments from authority. Life is often lived in the subjunctive mood, providing a wonderful excuse for poor prose. The academic protocols learned as a student can be shaped into a neat coiffure that one can wear under the scholar's hood if one is fortunate enough to get paid to think for a living. The baldness of writing these little essays was something that I had to get used to. I had the learn the art of the philosophical short cut.

Here I have been greatly aided by the person who has edited every word in this book, Peter Catapano (who has great hair), and who always wanted my writing to be balder, more direct and honest, when I wanted to conceal matters under a hirsute mat of words. Most, if not all, of the essays in this book have been the outcome of a fight over prose with Peter; a fight which, I am happy to say, I invariably lost because of his better sense of the economy and directness of expression. The essays in this book are the outgrowth of The Stone, the philosophy column in *The New York Times,* which Peter and I plotted, planned and launched in 2010. Working with Peter on The Stone has been one of the great adventures in my life and shown that there is indeed a large audience for philosophy as long as the writing is clear, crisp and free of jargon and has a point to make.

Academic writing can look hard to produce, intimidating even. This is often intentional and disguises much obviousness of thought. Once one has passed through the various rites of passage, like acquiring a PhD, and gained access to the guild of professional philosophers (and professional philosophy is rather like a medieval guild with masters, mistresses and apprentices being duly and dully trained), then one can mouth the words and write articles and books that follow a predictably dreary pattern of supposed academic rigor, which can sometimes stiffen into rigor mortis. Writing short essays for a newspaper can be harder than academic writing because of the baldness of expression and the limitations of the form, especially the word limit. There is no space for academic wigs or comb-overs. One has to stick one's bald head out of the window and speak.

Although it might seem that I'm talking myself out of my day job, there is a kind of comfort to the classroom, and however much I might think I am generating open, critical debate, a teacher's voice tends to dominate discussion. By contrast, writing for a newspaper can be unsettling because writers are legion, they are really good at writing and they don't really care about the relative height of your academic perch. One has to be bold and a little bald.

In our time, doing philosophy in public means sticking one's head out of the window and confronting and engaging the fluid, ambiguous and frenetic nature of the digital agora. For those of us more used to paper-bound publishing and waits of months or years for some sort of response—if there is any response at all—online publishing can be a thrilling but bewildering experience. The extraordinary speed and geographical reach of the online medium, with assent or criticism pouring in from readers within minutes of publication, takes getting used to. Of course, a shining, glabrous scalp represents an ideal target for virtual seagulls and sundry other creatures flying in cyberspace. If you stick your head out the window, something foul-smelling is likely to land on it.

But in looking back at these essays and assembling them into the more traditional form of a book, I have been constantly reminded of the countless acts of unsolicited kindness from readers, who have taken the time to write and who have responded generously to what I have written. I have learned a lot. Despite certain appearances to the contrary—Descartes seated next to his stove in the Low Countries, Wittgenstein in his Norwegian cabin or indeed Nietzsche in his rented rooms in Turin—philosophy is not a solitary activity of cogitation or rumination. In the various schools of antiquity, philosophy was a collective activity conducted in the Academy, the Lyceum of Aristotle, the Garden of Epicurus or the shade cast by the stoa.

It is difficult to find a stoa large enough for us all to fit these days, so our digital cave will have to suffice. But the point is that philosophy is a shared activity, it is dialogue. And dialogue is not the simple exchange of opinions, where I have my faith, my politics and my God and you have yours. That is parallel monologue. One of the goals of dialogue is to have our opinions rationally challenged in such a way that we might change our minds. True dialogue is changing one's mind. Thanks to the response that I have been fortunate enough to receive over the years, I know I've changed my mind. Many times.

The essays in this book are all date-stamped with the moment of their publication but not, I think, dated. From the get-go, my writing has usually been deliberately remote from the relentlessness of the day-to-day news cycle. I am not a political commentator and do not really have many interesting opinions. I have stretched the limits of the op-ed as much as Peter would let me get away with, and my use of the form has developed over the years into something much more oblique, observational and descriptive. The essays are not organized chronologically but have been sifted into categories (happiness, religion, philosophy, and so forth, ending with a coda on Covid-19) intended to make them more engaging to approach. Readers are naturally free to read them in sequence or jump around as they wish. I have had the immense good fortune to be able to use *The New York Times* as a laboratory for exploring ideas, sometimes odd ideas, some of which ended up in my books but many of which didn't. The discipline of writing for a newspaper and working closely with an editor has obliged me to shape and shave lines of thought, to aspire to accessible and jargon-free dialogue. My hope is simply that the writing is bald, in the sense of being the work of a naked, uncovered head.

Happiness?

1

Happy Like God

May 25, 2009

What is happiness? How does one get a grip on this elusive, intractable and perhaps most unanswerable of questions?

I teach philosophy for a living, so let me begin with a philosophical answer. For the philosophers of antiquity, notably Aristotle, it was assumed that the goal of the philosophical life—the good life, moreover—was happiness and that the good life could be defined as the *bios theoretikos*, the solitary life of contemplation. Today, few people would seem to subscribe to this view. Our lives are filled with the endless distractions of cell phones, car alarms, commuter woes and the traffic in Bangalore. The rhythm of modern life is punctuated by beeps and bleeps and interrupted by a generalized attention deficit disorder.

But is the idea of happiness as an experience of contemplation really so ridiculous? Might there not be something in it? I am reminded of the following extraordinary passage from Rousseau's final book and his third (count them—he still beats Obama 3 to 2) autobiography, *Reveries of a Solitary Walker:*

If there is a state where the soul can find a resting-place secure enough to establish itself and concentrate its entire being there, with no need to remember the past or reach into the future, where *time is nothing to it*, where the present runs on indefinitely but this duration goes unnoticed, with no sign of the passing of time, and no other feeling of deprivation or enjoyment, pleasure or pain, desire or fear than the simple *feeling of existence*, a feeling that fills our soul entirely, as long as this state lasts, we can call ourselves happy, not with a poor, incomplete and relative happiness such as we find in the pleasures of life, but with a sufficient, complete and perfect happiness which leaves no emptiness to be filled in the soul. [Emphases mine.]

This is as close to a description of happiness as I can imagine. Rousseau is describing the experience of floating in a little rowing boat on the Lake of Bienne close to Neuchâtel in his native Switzerland. He particularly loved visiting the Île Saint-Pierre, where he enjoyed going for exploratory walks when the weather was fine and he could indulge in the great passion of his last years: botany. He would walk with a copy of Linnaeus under his arm, happily identifying plants in areas of the deserted island that he had divided for this purpose into small squares.

On the way to the island, he would pull in the oars and let the boat drift for hours at a time. Rousseau would lie down in the boat and plunge into a deep reverie. How does one describe the experience of reverie: one is awake but half asleep, thinking but not in an instrumental, calculative or ordered way, simply letting the thoughts happen as they will.

Happiness is not quantitative or measurable, and it is not the object of any science, old or new. It cannot be gleaned from empirical surveys or programmed into individuals through a combination of behavioral therapy and antidepressants. If it consists in anything, I think that happiness is this *feeling of existence*, this sentiment of momentary self-sufficiency that is bound up with the experience of time

Look again at what Rousseau writes. Floating in a boat in fine weather, lying down with one's eyes open to the clouds and birds or closed in reverie, one does not feel the pull of the past, nor does one reach into the future. Time is nothing, or rather, time is nothing but the experience of the present through which one passes without hurry but without regret. As Wittgenstein writes in what must be the most intriguing remark in the *Tractatus*, "The eternal life is given to those who live in the present." Or, as Whitman writes in *Leaves of Grass:* "Happiness is not in another place, but in this place . . . not for another hour . . . but this hour."

Rousseau asks, "What is the source of our happiness in such a state?" He answers that it is nothing external to us and nothing apart from our own existence. However frenetic our environment, such a feeling of existence can be achieved. He goes on, amazingly, to conclude, "As long as this state lasts we are self-sufficient like God."

God-like, then. To which one might reply: Who? Me? Us? Like God? Dare we? But think about it: If anyone is happy, then one imagines that God is pretty happy, and to be happy is to be like God. But consider what this means, for it might not be as ludicrous, hubristic or heretical as one might imagine. To be like God is to be without time or, rather, in time with no concern for time, free of the passions and troubles of the soul, experiencing something like calm in the face of things and oneself.

Why should happiness be bound up with the presence and movement of water? This is the case for Rousseau, and I must confess that if I think back over those experiences of blissful reverie that are close to what Rousseau is describing, I realize they often took place in proximity to water, though usually saltwater rather than fresh. For me, it is not so much the stillness of a lake (I tend to see lakes as decaffeinated seas) as the neverending drone of the surf as I sit by the sea in fair weather or foul and feel time disappear into tide, into the endless pendulum of the tidal chronometer. At moments like this, one can sink into deep reverie, a motionlessness that is not sleep, but where one is somehow held by the sound of the surf, lulled by the tidal movement.

Is all happiness solitary? Of course not. But one can be happy alone, and this might even be the key to being happy with others. Wordsworth wandered lonely as a cloud when walking with his sister. However, I think that one can also experience this feeling of existence in the experience of love, in being intimate with one's lover, feeling the world close around one and time slipping away in its passing. Rousseau's rowing boat becomes the lovers' bed, and one bids the world farewell while sliding into the shared selfishness of intimacy.

. . . And then it is over. Time passes, the reverie ends and the feeling for existence fades. The cell phone rings, the email beeps and one is sucked back into the world's relentless hum and the accompanying anxiety.

2

Beyond the Sea

May 29, 2009

Thinking is thanking. So let me begin by thanking the readers of "Happy Like God" for their thoughtful and voluminous responses. It is obviously impossible to do justice to the range of the many responses or indeed assuage the outrage that my words seemed to inspire in some. But several interconnected themes were echoed in many of the comments, and I'd like to address some of them.

Before I begin, let me state the obvious: There is no one-size-fits-all recipe for happiness, and it would be truly dreadful if there were. Therefore, although I am happy that many people agree with me, I am even happier that some disagree.

Aside from being a literary genius, Rousseau is a difficult character to love, and many comments picked up on that fact. Aside from dumping his five children in a foundling hospital, Jean-Jacques was self-obsessed and totally paranoid. Given the chance, I would much rather spend an evening in the company of David Hume, one of Rousseau's erstwhile enemies. Hume's autobiographical essay covers barely ten pages, and begins, "It is difficult for a man to speak long of himself without vanity;

therefore, I shall be short." Such was Rousseau's vanity that he spoke very long of himself and wrote three autobiographies. This is not the place to ruminate on the details of Jean-Jacques's sexual masochism as described in the *Confessions*, or his bizarre dialogue with himself in *Rousseau, Critic of Jean-Jacques*, which he deposited on the altar at Notre Dame in Paris. But it is Rousseau's endlessly tortured vanity that makes the moment of bliss in his little boat on the Lake of Bienne so arresting, so utterly surprising. After the storm of lacerating misery, self-justification and self-critique described in his first two autobiographies, Rousseau achieves a calm of sorts in *Reveries*, a simple feeling of existence bound up with the experience of water.

Many readers quibbled with the priority given to water, particularly saltwater, in my piece. Some preferred mountains, others delighted in the desert, and one reader praised the illicit experience of foraging and trespassing over my love of things maritime. I'm not fussy. I think the feeling of existence I tried to describe can happen in all sorts of places: during a momentary distraction on the street, at the sound of birdsong in a break in car traffic, even in the subway as one's head lifts from a newspaper to see the Q train crossing the Manhattan Bridge at sunset. But I believe that there is a special connection between meditation and water.

Think of the beginning of *Moby-Dick*, where Melville describes the "insular city of the Manhattoes belted round by wharves as Indian isles by coral reefs—commerce surrounds it with her surf." Even here, in the entirely mercantile, commercial bustle of mid-nineteenth-century New York, Melville observes "thousands upon thousands of mortal men fixed in ocean reveries." These are what he calls the "water-gazers," inlanders all, desperate to stand close to the water, "They must get just as nigh the water as they possibly can." Melville goes on—as only Melville can—to ponder the connection between human beings and the sea: "Why did the old Persians hold the sea holy? Why did the Greeks give it a separate deity?" He concludes that we witness something mysterious about ourselves and our origins in the contemplation of the sea, something vast, sublime and incomprehensible. He writes, "It is the image of the ungraspable phantom of life."

I was delighted that one reader recalled Beckett's *Krapp's Last Tape*, which is a hugely important play to my mind, much more so than *Waiting for Godot*. The wizened, elderly Krapp listens obsessively to the recorded voice of a younger version of himself, who is both more hopeful and more idiotic. The portion of tape to which he listens repeatedly offers an epiphanal moment with a lover while punting on a lake:

> I lay down across her with my face in her breasts
> and my hand on her. We lay there without moving.
> But under us all moved, and moved us, gently, up
> and down, and from side to side.

This passage raises two points that came up in some of the comments. Firstly, Krapp's experience of bliss is shared with another, with a former lover. This addresses the criticism that Rousseau's picture of happiness was solitary, indeed selfish and narcissistic. Well, narcissism is a complicated matter, and we should not forget that after obsessively contemplating his image in water, Narcissus drowned himself. But the point is well taken, and I tried to acknowledge it at the end of the piece: the feeling for existence can be had with others. Perhaps it is best had with others in the experience of love, whether it is love of another person, as for Krapp, or of one's cats and dogs, as came up more than once in the comments, or indeed in the experience of being face to face with a tiger, as one reader wrote.

Secondly, the passage from Beckett reminds us that this transient experience of bliss is a recollected experience, a work of memory. This is the lost time that we go in search of. It is one thing to experience happiness in the moment; it is another to recall such memories months, years or even decades later. This is one of the reasons why we feel compelled to write at all. Rousseau's reverie on the little boat is recollected long after the fact. I don't think this is just nostalgia; it is rather the experience of what the Portuguese and Brazilians call *saudade,* a kind of longing, a desire to recall something lost. But true saudade accepts— almost fatalistically—the fact that the moment of bliss has passed. This is why happiness is never fully distinguishable from the experience of melancholy, nor should it be. Perhaps we might say that happiness recalled is more intense than happiness experienced because it is tinged with longing and melancholy.

One reader rightly points out that happiness is not a question of time's absence, which is absurd, but rather of the intensity of a certain experience of time. To say, as Rousseau does, that the state of bliss is one "where time is nothing to it" is not to say that there is no time. It is a question of a different experience of the present, what Heidegger calls the rapture of ecstatic time that breaks through the ordinary series of past, present and future that habitually marks the rhythm of our lives. If eternity means anything, it is this lived intensity of the present.

An issue that came up in many of the comments was the relation between contemplation and action and the privilege that I seem to give to the former over the latter. Firstly, I would respond that contemplation is action (there is nothing passive about thinking), and action is sometimes contemplative (when I do not lose myself in thoughtless action but think along with the act I undertake). But I concede that where Rousseau, Beckett or Melville might find this feeling for existence in bodily stillness, others might find it in vigorous physical activity. Nietzsche once said that all truly great thoughts are conceived while walking.

And yes, wonderful as they are, and although I am far from a Luddite, I do regret the ways our lives have become punctuated through the constant use of cell phones and other multiple media platforms. We risk becoming people, in Eliot's words, distracted from distraction by distraction. Ours is a culture defined by attention deficit disorder. What some readers saw as selfishness in Rousseau is, I think, more properly described as the attempt to cultivate a space and time of attention to things, to things in their wonderful variousness and plurality. To cultivate this discipline of attention is, I think, to press back against the pressure of reality, to produce with words and thoughts felt variations in the appearances of things.

There is no happiness machine, nor should there be. Happiness is not a quantitative matter. It is a matter of the quality of one's life and in what that quality consists. The most painful but also the most joyous response came from Robert F., who is faced with terminal brain cancer. I'd like to end with what he writes, in an echo of Epicurus:

If you're religious, what's beyond the act of dying is a better place; if you're not religious, there is nothing. In either case there's no need to worry. What matters is the journey between right now and that event.

3
How to Make It in the Afterlife

June 23, 2009

I am writing from Athens, doing what might loosely be described as work, with some rather bad news. Just when you thought it couldn't get any worse—you've lost your job, your retirement portfolio has been exfoliated, Bernie Madoff has made off with your money, your pet cat Jeoffrey has left you for a neighbor and economic recession has become psychological depression—you discover the awful truth: you're going to die.

Somehow, it was always expected, always certain, along with taxes. You'd even smiled weakly at that old dictum. Now and then you had heard time's wingèd chariot drawing near, but had put it down to street noise and returned to your daily round of labor, leisure and slumber. Now, stripped of the usual diversions and evasions of life, the realization begins to dawn: no matter how healthily you eat or how much you deny your sedentary desires in the name of fitness, no matter how many sacrifices you make to the great god of longevity, you are going to die. Sooner or later you are going to become worm food— unless, of course, you choose cremation.

What, then, might be the relation between happiness and death? As is so often the case, the ancient Greeks had a powerful thought, which to us today seems counterintuitive: "Call no man happy until he is dead." What is the meaning of this remark, often attributed to Solon but different versions of which can be found in Aeschylus and Herodotus?

The idea here is that one can be sure that one's life is happy only when it has come to an end. No matter how nobly one might have lived, however much courage one had shown in battle, however diligently one had served as a public citizen or privately as a paterfamilias in the rather patriarchal structure of ancient Greek family life, there was still the risk that life could end badly. One could die ignominiously or, even worse, in a cowardly or ludicrous manner: Heraclitus suffocated in cow dung; Xenocrates died after tripping over a bronze utensil in the night; Chrysippus died laughing after seeing an old woman feed figs to an ass. For the ancient Greeks, a life lived well was a life rounded off, consummated even, in a noble or appropriate death.

This means that happiness does not consist in whatever you might be feeling—after death, of course, you might not be feeling much at all—but in what others feel about you. It consists more precisely in the stories that can be told about you after your death. This is what the Greeks called glory, and it expresses a very different understanding of immortality than is common among us today. One lives on only through the stories, accounts and anecdotes that are told about one. It is in this that happiness consists.

In societies like ours in the United States, so singlemindedly devoted to the pursuit of happiness, we assume that the question of happiness is a question of *my* happiness or, more properly, of *my* relation to *my* happiness. But why? Why doesn't it make much better sense to live in such a way—to act kindly, fairly, courageously, decently—that happiness is something that others might ascribe to you after you are gone?

Having recently written a book on how philosophers die, and being a philosophy teacher myself (and yes, I too will die at some point. I am quite sure of it), I am often asked the question, "Do you believe in the afterlife?" After mumbling something stupid on a few occasions, I have now learned to reply, "Yes, of course I believe in the afterlife. I believe in the life of those that come after, those we love, who are few in number, and those we don't even know, who are obviously a great many in number." People rarely seem impressed by this answer.

But why should we assume that the question of the afterlife must always be answered with reference to *me?* Isn't that just a teensy bit selfish? What is so important about *my* afterlife? Why can't I believe in the afterlife of others without believing in my own?

A skeptic might object that I am dodging the question. Of course, they might say, the question of the afterlife is about *your* afterlife. So, does it go on or not, this series of disconnected events that we call existence?

The only really philosophical reply I can give is, "I don't know."

After he had been condemned to death on the trumped-up charges of corrupting the youth of Athens and failing to revere the local gods, Socrates ruminated on the afterlife before an audience of his judges.

He said that death is one of two possibilities. Either it is a long dreamless sleep and really rather pleasant, or it is a passage to another place, namely Hades, where we'll be able to hang out with Homer, Hesiod and rest of the Greek heroes, which sounds great. Socrates's point is that we do not know whether death is the end or some sort of continuation. He concludes by saying only God knows the answer to this question. This makes it tricky if you don't, like me, have the good fortune to believe in God.

4

The Gospel According to Me

WITH JAMIESON WEBSTER

June 29, 2013

The booming self-help industry, not to mention the cash cow of New Age spirituality, has one message: Be authentic! Charming as American optimism may be, its twenty-first-century incarnation as the search for authenticity deserves a pause for thought. The power of this new version of the American dream can be felt through the stridency of its imperatives: Live fully! Realize yourself! Be connected! Achieve well-being!

Despite the frequent claim that we are living in a secular age defined by the death of God, many citizens in rich Western democracies have merely switched one notion of God for another—abandoning their singular, omnipotent (Christian or Judaic or whatever) deity who reigns over all humankind and replacing it with a weak but all-pervasive idea of spirituality tied to a personal ethic of authenticity and a liturgy of inwardness. This idea does not make the exorbitant moral demands of traditional religions, which impose bad conscience, guilt, sin, sexual inhibition and the rest.

Unlike the conversions that transfigure the born-again's experience of the world in a lightning strike, this one occurred in stages: a postwar existentialist philosophy of personal liberation and "becoming who you are" fed into a 1960s counterculture that mutated into selfish conformism, which disguises acquisitiveness under a patina of personal growth, mindfulness and compassion. Traditional forms of morality that required extensive social cooperation in relation to a hard reality defined by scarcity have largely collapsed and been replaced with this New Age therapeutic culture of well-being that does not require obedience or even faith—and certainly not feelings of guilt. Guilt must be shed; alienation, both of body and mind, must be eliminated, most notably through yoga practice after a long day of mind-numbing work.

In the gospel of authenticity, well-being has become the primary goal of human life. Rather than being the by-product of some collective project, some upbuilding of the New Jerusalem, well-being is an end in itself. The stroke of genius in the ideology of authenticity is that it doesn't really require a belief in anything, and certainly not a belief in anything that might transcend the serene and contented living of one's authentic life. In this, one can claim to be beyond dogma.

Whereas the American dream used to be tied to external reality—say, America as the place where one can openly practice any religion, America as a safe haven from political oppression or America as the land of opportunity where one need not struggle as hard as one's parents did—now the dream is one of pure psychological transformation.

This phenomenon one might call, with an appreciative nod to Nietzsche, passive nihilism. Authenticity is its dominant contemporary expression. In a seemingly meaningless, inauthentic world awash in nonstop media reports of war, violence and inequality, we close our eyes and turn ourselves into islands.

We may even say a little prayer to an obscure but benign Eastern goddess and feel some weak spiritual energy connecting everything as we listen to some tastefully selected ambient music. Authenticity, needing no reference to anything outside itself, is an evacuation of history. The power of now.

This ideology functions prominently in the contemporary workplace, where the classical distinction between work and nonwork has broken down. Work was traditionally seen as a curse or an obligation for which we received payment. Nonwork was viewed as an experience of freedom for which we paid but which gave us pleasure.

But the past thirty years or so has ushered in an informalization of the workplace, where the distinction between work and nonwork is harder and harder to draw. With the rise of corporations like Google, the workplace has increasingly been colonized by nonwork experiences to the extent that we are not allowed to feel alienation or discontent at the office because we can play Ping-Pong, ride a Segway and eat organic lunches from a menu designed by celebrity chefs. If we do feel discontent, something must be wrong with us rather than with the corporation.

With the workplace dominated by the maxim of personal authenticity—Be different! Wear your favorite T-shirt to work and listen to Radiohead on your iPhone while at your desk! Isn't it nifty?—there is no room for worker malaise. And contrary to popular belief, none of this has assuaged the workplace dynamics of guilt, bad conscience and anxiety, which are more rampant than ever. In fact, the blurring of the boundary between work and nonwork in the name of flexibility has led to an enormous increase in anxiety—a trend well documented in the work of Peter Fleming, a professor of work, organization and society at the University of London. Women in particular feel totally inadequate for not being able to have it all—climb the ladder at work, make the same wages as men, have a family, have a voluminous sex life, still look attractive—and they have to act as if they are having a great time nonetheless.

Work is no longer a series of obligations to be fulfilled for the sake of sustenance: it is the expression of one's authentic self. With the extraordinary rise of internships—not just filled by college students anymore, but more and more by working-age adults—people from sufficiently privileged backgrounds are even prepared to work without pay because it allows them to "grow" as persons. Every aspect of one's existence is meant to water some fantasy of growth.

But here's the rub: If one believes that there is an intimate connection between one's authentic self and glittering success at work, then the experience of failure and forced unemployment is accepted as one's own fault. I feel shame for losing my job. I am morally culpable for the corporation's decision that I am excess to requirements.

To take this one step further: the failure of others is explained by their merely partial enlightenment, for which they, and they alone, are to be held responsible. At the heart of the ethic of authenticity is a profound selfishness and callous disregard of others. As New Age interpreters of Buddha affirm, "You yourself, as much as anybody in the entire universe, deserve your love and affection."

A naive belief in authenticity eventually gives way to a deep cynicism. A conviction that personal success must always hold failure at bay becomes a corrupt stubbornness that insists on success at any cost. Cynicism, in this mode, is not the expression of a critical stance toward authenticity but is rather the runoff of this failure of belief. The self-help industry itself runs the gamut in both directions—from *The Power of Now*, which teaches the power of meditative self-sufficiency, to *The Rules*, which teaches a woman how to land a man by pretending to be self-sufficient. Profit rules the day, inside and out.

Nothing seems more American than this forced choice between cynicism and naive belief. Or rather, as Herman Melville put it in his 1857 novel, *The Confidence Man,* the choice is between being a fool (having to believe what one says) or being a knave (saying things one does not believe). For Melville, who was writing on the cusp of modern capitalism, the search for authenticity was a white whale.

This search is an obsession that is futile at best and destructive at worst. The lingering question for Melville, on the brink of poverty as he wrote *The Confidence Man,* was: What happens to charity? When the values of Judeo-Christian morality have been given a monetary and psychological incarnation—as in credit, debt, trust, faith and fidelity—can they exist as values? Is the prosperous self the only God in which we believe in a radically inauthentic world?

As usual, the Bard of Avon got there first. In *Hamlet,* Shakespeare puts the mantra of authenticity into the mouth of the ever-idiotic windbag Polonius in his advice to his son, Laertes: "To thine own self be true." This is just before Polonius sends a spy to follow Laertes to Paris and tell any number of lies to catch him out.

And who, finally, is more inauthentic than Hamlet? Ask yourself: Is Hamlet true to himself, doubting everything, unable to avenge his father's murder, incapable of uttering the secret that he has learned from the ghost's lips, and unwilling to declare his love for Ophelia, whose father he kills? Hamlet dies wearing the colors of his enemy, Claudius. We dare say that we love *Hamlet,* not for its representation of our purportedly sublime authenticity, but as a depiction of the drama of our radical inauthenticity that, in the best of words and worlds, shatters our moral complacency.

5
Abandon (Nearly) All Hope

April 19, 2014

With Easter upon us, powerful narratives of rebirth and resurrection are in the air and on the breeze. However, winter's stubborn reluctance to make way for the pleasing and hopeful season leads me to think not of cherry blossoms and Easter Bunnies but of Prometheus, Nietzsche, Barack Obama and the very roots of hope. Is hope always such a wonderful thing? Is it not rather a form of moral cowardice that allows us to escape from reality and prolong human suffering?

Prometheus the Titan was punished by the Olympian Zeus by being chained to a rock in the Caucasus, quite possibly not that far from Crimea. Each day an eagle pecked out his liver. Every night the liver grew back. An unpleasant situation, I'm sure you would agree. His transgression was to have given human beings the gift of fire and, with that, the capacity for craft, technological inventiveness and what we are fond of calling civilization.

This is well known. Less well known is Prometheus's second gift. In Aeschylus's *Prometheus Bound*, the chained Titan is pitilessly interrogated by the chorus. They ask him whether he gave human beings anything else. "Yes," he says, "I stopped mortals from foreseeing doom." "How did you do that?" they ask. His response is revealing: "I sowed in them blind hopes."

This is a very Greek thought. It stands resolutely opposed to Christianity, with its trinity of faith, love and hope. For Saint Paul—Christianity's true founder, it must be recalled—hope is both a moral attitude of steadfastness and a hope for what is laid up in heaven for us, namely salvation. This is why faith in the resurrection of Jesus Christ is so absolutely fundamental to Christians. Christ died on the cross, but he was resurrected and lives eternally. Jesus is our hope, as Paul writes in the First Letter to Timothy; he is the basis for the faith that we too might live eternally. Heaven, as they say, is real.

In his Letter to the Romans, Paul inadvertently confirms Prometheus's gift of blind hope. He asserts that hope in what is seen is not hope at all, "For who hopes for what he sees?" On the contrary, we should "hope for what we do not see" and "wait for it with patience."

Now, fast-forward to us. When Barack Obama describes how he came to write his keynote speech for the 2004 Democratic National Convention, the speech that instantly shot him to fame and laid the basis for his presidential campaign and indeed his presidency, he recalls a phrase that his pastor, the Reverend Jeremiah A. Wright Jr., used in a sermon: the audacity of hope. Obama says that this audacity is what "was the best of the American spirit," namely "the audacity to believe despite all the evidence to the contrary."

It is precisely this kind of hope that I think we should try to give up. It is not audacious but mendacious. As the wise Napoleon said, "A leader is a dealer in hope" who governs by insisting on a bright outlook despite all evidence to the contrary. But what if we looked at matters differently? What if we expected more from political life than a four-yearly trade-in of

our moral intelligence to one or other of the various hope deal-
ers who appear on the political market to sell us some shiny
new vehicle of salvation?

The problem here is with the way in which this audacious
Promethean theological idea of hope has migrated into our
national psyche to such an extent that it blinds us to the reality
of the world that we inhabit and causes a sort of sentimental
complacency that prevents us from seeing things aright and
protesting against this administration's moral and political
lapses and those of other administrations.

Against the inflated and finally hypocritical rhetoric of
contemporary politics, I think it is instructive to look at things
from another standpoint, an ancient and very Greek standpoint.
Just as our stories shape us as citizens, their stories shaped them
and might shape us too. So, let me tell you a story, perhaps the
most terrifying from antiquity.

In *The History of the Peloponnesian War*, Thucydides,
the sober and unsentimental historian, describes a dialogue
between the representatives of the island of Melos in the Ae-
gean Sea, which was allied with Sparta, and some ambassadors
from invading Athenian military forces. The ambassadors present the Melians with a very simple choice: Submit to us or be
destroyed.

Rather than submit, the Melians wriggle. They express
hope that the Spartans will come to rescue them. The Athenians
calmly point out that it would be an extremely dangerous mis-
sion for the Spartans to undertake and was highly unlikely to
happen. Also, they add, rightly, "We are masters of the sea." The
Spartans had formidable land forces but were no match for the
Athenian navy.

The Melians plead that if they yield to the Athenians, all
hope will be lost. If they continue to hold out, "we can still hope
to stand tall." The Athenians reply that it is indeed true that

hope *is* a great comfort, but often a delusive one. They add that the Melians will learn what hope is when it fails them, "for hope is prodigal by nature."

With consummate clarity and no small cruelty, the Athenians urge the Melians not to turn to Promethean blind hopes when they are forced to give up their sensible ones. Reasonable hopes can soon become unreasonable. "Do not be like ordinary people," they add, "who could use human means to save themselves but turn to blind hopes when they are forced to give up their sensible ones—to divination, oracles and other such things that destroy men by giving them hope."

At this point, the Athenians withdraw and leave the Melians to consider their position. As usually happens in political negotiations, the Melians decide to stick to exactly the same position that they had adopted before the debate. They explain that "we will trust in the fortune of the Gods." In a final statement, the Athenians conclude, "You have staked everything on your trust in hope . . . and you will be ruined in everything."

After laying siege to the Melian city and skirmishing back and forth, the Athenians lose patience with the Melians and, as Thucydides reports with breathtaking understatement, "They killed all the men of military age and made slaves of the women and children."

Thucydides offers no moral commentary on the Melian Dialogue. He does not tell us how to react but instead impartially presents us with a real situation. The dialogue is an argument from power about the nature of power. This is why Nietzsche, in his polemics against Christianity and liberalism, loved Thucydides. This is also why I love Nietzsche. Should one reproach Thucydides for describing the negotiations between the Athenians and the Melians without immediately moralizing and telling us how we should think? Not at all, Nietzsche insists.

What we witness in the Melian Dialogue is the true character of Greek *realism*.

Elected regimes can become authoritarian, democracies can become corrupted, and invading armies usually behave abominably. What we need in the face of what Nietzsche calls "a strict, hard factuality" is not hope but "*courage* in the face of reality."

For Nietzsche, the alternative to Thucydides is Plato. With his usual lack of moderation, Nietzsche declares that Platonism is cowardice in the face of reality because it constructs fictional metaphysical ideals like justice, virtue and the good. Nietzsche sees Platonism as a flight from the difficulty of reality into a vapid moralistic idealism. Furthermore, he adds, we have been stuck with versions of moral idealism ever since Plato, notably in Christianity, with its hope in salvation, and modern liberalism, with its trust in God and its insistence, contrary to all evidence, on hope's audacity.

Where does this leave us? Rather than see Thucydides as an apologist for authoritarianism, I see him as a deep but disappointed democrat with a clear-eyed view of democracy's limitations, particularly when Athens voted to engage in misplaced military adventures like the disastrous expedition to Sicily that led to Sparta's final victory over Athens in the Peloponnesian War. Thucydides would doubtless have had a similar view of the United States' military expeditions to countries like Afghanistan and Iraq on the basis of metaphysical abstractions like enduring freedom or infinite justice. But he would have thought it was even worse for democracies to speak out of both sides of their mouths, offering vigorous verbal support for invaded or embattled peoples and talking endlessly of freedom and hope while doing precisely nothing.

When democracy goes astray, as it always will, the remedy should not be an idealistic belief in hope's audacity, which ends up sounding either cynical or dogmatic, or both. The remedy, in my view, is a skeptical realism, deeply informed by history. Such realism has an abiding commitment to reason and the need for negotiation and persuasion, but also an acute awareness of reason's limitations in the face of violence and belligerence. As Thucydides realized long before the 2004 Democratic National Convention, it is not difficult to make beautiful speeches in politics, but speeches very often do little to change people's minds and effect palpable improvement in social arrangements.

Thinking without hope might sound rather bleak, but it needn't be. I see it as embracing an affirmative, even cheerful realism. Nietzsche admired Epictetus, the former slave turned philosophy teacher, for living without hope. "Yes," Nietzsche said, "he can smile." We can too.

You can have all kinds of reasonable hopes, it seems to me, the modest, pragmatic and indeed deliberately fuzzy kinds of social hope expressed by an anti-Platonist philosopher like Richard Rorty. But unless those hopes are realistic, we will end up with a blindly hopeful (and therefore hopeless) idealism. Prodigal hope invites despair only when we see it fail. In giving up the former, we might also avoid the latter. This is not an easy task, I know. But we should try. Nietzsche writes, "Hope is the evil of evils because it prolongs man's torment." By clinging to hope we often make the suffering worse.

I Believe

6

Why I Love Mormonism

September 16, 2012

I've spent what is rapidly becoming nine years in New York City. It's been a total blast. But as a transplanted Englishman, I've become rather sensitive to one thing: which prejudices New Yorkers are permitted to express in public. Among my horribly overeducated and hugely liberal friends, expressions of racism are completely out of the question, Islamophobia is greeted with a slow shaking of the head and anti-Semitism is a memory associated with distant places that one sometimes visits—like France.

But anti-Mormonism is another matter. It's socially acceptable to say totally uninformed things about Mormonism in public, at dinner parties or wherever. "It's a cult," says one. "With thirteen million followers and counting?" I reply. "Polygamy is disgusting," says another. "It was made illegal in Utah and banned by the church in 1890, wasn't it?" I counter. And so on. This is a casual prejudice. It is not like the visceral hatred that plagued the early decades of Mormonism—lest it be forgotten, Joseph Smith was shot to death on June 27, 1844, by an angry mob who broke into a jail where he was detained—but a symptom of a thoughtless incuriousness.

There is just something weird about Mormonism, and the very mention of the Book of Mormon invites smirks and giggles, which is why choosing it as the name for Broadway's most hard-to-get-into show was a smart move. As a scholar of Mormonism once remarked, one does not need to read the Book of Mormon in order to have an opinion about it.

But every now and then during one of those New York soirées, when anti-Mormon prejudice is persistently pressed and expressed, and I perhaps feel momentarily and un-Mormonly emboldened by wine, I try to share my slim understanding of Joseph Smith and my fascination with the Latter-day Saints. After about forty-five seconds, sometimes less, it becomes apparent that the expressed prejudice was based on sheer ignorance of the peculiar splendors of Mormon theology. "They are all Republicans anyway," they add in conclusion. "I mean, just look at that Mitbot Romney. He's an alien." As an alien myself, I find this thoughtless anti-Mormon sentiment bewildering.

This is mainly because of my direct experience with Mormonism. Very early on in my philosophical travels, near the Italian city of Perugia, to be precise, I met Mormon philosophers—Heideggerians actually, but this was the 1980s, when many such dinosaurs roamed the earth—and got to know them quite well. They were from Brigham Young University, and they were some of the kindest, most self-effacing and honest people I have ever met. They were also funny, warm, genuine, completely open-minded, smart and terribly well read. We became friends.

There was still suspicion, of course, perhaps even more so back then. I remember being pulled aside late at night by an American friend and told, "You know that guy from BYU. They say he's a bishop and conducts secret services." "Does he eat babies too?" I wondered out loud.

Thereby hangs a story. Because of my convivial contact
with these philosophers from Brigham Young University I was
invited in 1994 to give a series of lectures. I stayed for more
than a week in Provo, Utah. The absence of caffeine or any
other stimulants was tough, but the hospitality was fulsome,
and I was welcomed into people's homes and treated with great
civility and care. My topic was Romanticism, and the argument
kicked off from the idea that the extraordinary burst of creative
energy that we associate with Romantic poetry comes out of a
disappointment with a religious, specifically Christian, worldview. Poetry became secular scripture. In other words, Romantic art announced the death of God, an idea that caught fire in
the later nineteenth century. It's a familiar story.

Things went pretty well. But right at the end of the final
lecture, a member of the audience asked me an odd question.
He said, "What you have been telling us this week about Romanticism and the death of God where religion becomes art is
premised on a certain understanding of God, namely that God
is unitary and infinite. Would you agree?" "Sure," I said, "At least
two of the predicates of the divinity are that he/she/it is unitary
and infinite." Gosh, I was smart back then. "But what if," he
went on, "God were plural and finite?"

Concealing my slight shock, I simply said, "Pray tell."
Everyone in the room laughed knowingly. And with that the
chairman closed the session. I went straight to my questioner
and pleaded, "Tell me more." Thirty minutes later, over a caf-
feine-free Diet Coke in the university cafeteria, he explained
what lay behind his question.

"You see," my questioner said, "in his late sermons, Joseph
Smith developed some really radical ideas. For a start, God did
not create space and time, but is subject to them and is therefore
a finite being. The Mormon God is somewhat hedged in by the
universe and is not master of it. The text to look at here is an

amazing sermon called 'King Follett,' which was named after
an elder who had just died, and was delivered in Nauvoo, Illi-
nois, a few months before the prophet was murdered. He asks
repeatedly, 'What kind of being is God?' And his reply is that
God himself was once as we are now."

He leaned in closer to me and continued in a lower voice,
"If you were to see God right now, Smith says, *right now,* you
would see a being just like you, the very form of a man. The
great secret is that, through heroic effort and striving, God was
a man who became exalted and now sits enthroned in the
heavens. You see, God was not God from all eternity but *became*
God. Now, the flip side of this claim is that if God is an exalted
man, then we, too, can become exalted. The prophet says to the
company of the saints something like, 'You have to learn how
to be gods. You have to inherit the same power and glory as
God and become exalted like him.' Namely you can arrive at
the station of God. One of our early leaders summarized the
King Follett sermon with the words, 'As man now is, God once
was. As God now is, man may be.' "

"So, dear Simon," my new friend concluded, "we, too, can
become Gods, American Gods, no less." He chuckled. I was
astonished.

My host, Jim, arrived to pick me up for an early dinner at
his home and then drove me back to Salt Late City to make a
late flight to Chicago. I kept looking at the vast night sky over
the Utah desert and thinking about what my interlocutor had
said. I read the King Follett sermon and anything else I could
find, particularly a very late sermon by Smith on the plurality
of Gods, given around ten days before the prophet's murder.
What I read totally blew me away. I also stole a copy of the Book
of Mormon from the Marriott Hotel in Chicago and waded
through as much of it as I could. To be honest, it's somewhat
tedious.

I knew that what the audience member had told me was heresy. Christianity is premised on the fact of the incarnation. There was a God-man rabbi in occupied Palestine a couple of millennia ago. But that doesn't mean that *anyone* can go around claiming divinity, like Joachim of Fiore in the twelfth century or the recently deceased and much missed Reverend Sun Myung Moon. There was only one incarnation. God became man, was crucified and resurrected, and we're still waiting for him to come back. The New Testament, especially the Book of Revelation, is very clear that he is coming soon. Admittedly, it's been a while.

To explain the consubstantiality of God and man in the person of Christ, third- and fourth-century Christian Fathers, including Saint Augustine, built up the wonderful theological edifice of the Trinity. The three persons of the Trinity, Father, Son and Holy Ghost, are distinct but participate in the same substance. Three in one is one in three. It is a heretical act of arrogance to arrogate divinity to oneself or to claim multiple incarnations. God is indeed unitary and infinite.

Joseph Smith believed none of that. He taught that God the Father and God the Son were separate substances, both of them material. Speaking directly of the Trinity, Smith remarked, "I say that is a strange God," and goes on, in a line that must have earned big laughs back in 1844, "It would make the biggest God in the world. He would be a wonderfully big God—he would be a giant or a monster." Not only is the Mormon God not as big as the Christian God, there are any number of Gods within Mormonism. In the late sermons, Smith repeatedly talks about a council of the Gods that took place sometime before the Book of Genesis begins. The existence of the council is based on a rather windy interpretation of various Hebrew words. Smith claims in conclusion: "The head God called together the Gods and sat in grand council to bring forth the world."

But wait, things get even weirder. Smith accepts that Jesus Christ had a father, namely God. "You may suppose that He had a Father," adding, "Was there ever a son without a father?" Common sense would answer no, but Christians must answer, "Yes, there was." That is, God created all creatures but was himself uncreated. God is *causa sui,* a self-caused cause. Smith, however, explicitly rejects this idea: "We say that God Himself is a self-existing being. Who told you so?" He goes on, "I might with boldness proclaim from the house-tops that God never had the power to create the spirit of man at all. God himself could not create himself." God is not an uncaused cause but is himself part of the chain of causation.

Something a little like that amazing exchange is said to have taken place following Bertrand Russell's lecture "Why I Am Not a Christian," given at Battersea Town Hall in South London in 1927. After Russell had made his case for atheism, a female questioner asked him, "What Mr. Russell has said is well enough, but he has forgotten that the entire universe stands on the back of a turtle." Quite unfazed, Russell answered, "Madam, upon what does the turtle stand?" "Oh," she said, "it's turtles all the way down."

For Joseph Smith, it is turtles all the way down. There is an endless regress of Gods who beget one another but who do not beget the universe. That is, creation is not ex nihilo, as it is in Christianity, where God created heaven and earth, as it says at the beginning of the Bible. Rather, matter precedes creation. This makes the Mormon God like the demiurge in Plato's pagan creation myth in the *Timeaus.* The Mormon God does not create matter. He organizes it. Admittedly, he organized it pretty impressively. Just look at the design of trees.

The great thing about Mormonism is that Mormons take very seriously the doctrine of incarnation. So seriously, indeed, that they have succeeded in partially democratizing it. For

Christians, incarnation is a one-time, long-distance ski jump from the divine to the human. But for Joseph Smith, incarnation is more of a two-way street and potentially a rather congested thoroughfare. If God becomes man, then man can become God. And the word "man" has to be understood literally here. Women cannot be priests or prophets or aspire to an exclusively masculine divinity, which seems petty, a pity, and rather silly to me. But there we are. And I don't even want to get into questions of race and the exclusion of blacks from the Mormon priesthood until 1978.

The point is that any number of Mormon men can become God—potentially even you know who. It's an intriguing thought.

There is a potential equality of the human and the divine within Mormonism, at least in the extraordinary theology that Joseph Smith speedily sketched in the King Follett sermon. Divinity is the object of that much-admired Mormon striving. Perhaps this is why so many Mormons are so hardworking.

Smith says, and one gets a clear sense of the persecution that he felt and that indeed engulfed and killed him, "They found fault with Jesus Christ because He said He was the Son of God, and made Himself equal with God. They say of me, like they did of the apostles of old, that I must be put down. What did Jesus say? 'Is it not written in your law, I said: Ye are Gods.' ... Why should it be blasphemy that I should say I am the Son of God."

Of course, for Christians, this is the highest blasphemy. But the Mormon vision is very distinctive. The idea is that within each of us is a spirit, what Smith calls an "intelligence," that is co-equal with God. Smith says in the King Follett sermon, "The first principles of man are self-existent with God." This intelligence is immortal. As Smith explicates, "There never was a time when there were not spirits, for they are co-equal (co-eternal) with our father in heaven." If God could not create himself, then one might say that each of us has within us something uncreated, something that precedes God and that is itself divine.

Having accepted being sent into the world, as Mormons sometimes put it, we have the task of exalting ourselves so that we, too, can become Gods. God the Father was just a stronger, more intelligent God capable of guiding weaker intelligences like us. As Smith says in a marvelously sensuous, indeed gustatory, turn of phrase, "This is good doctrine. It tastes good. I can taste the principles of eternal life, and so can you." Who wouldn't want a taste of God or to taste what it might be like to be a God oneself?

The heretical vistas of Mormonism, particularly the idea of something uncreated within the human being, excited the self-described Gnostic Jew Harold Bloom. I read his wonderful 1992 book, *The American Religion,* shortly after my trip to Utah and reread it recently with great pleasure. Bloom sees Mormonism as the quintessential expression of an American religion and controversially links the idea of the plurality of Gods to plural marriage. The argument is very simple: If you are or have the potential to become divine, and divinity is corporeal, then plural marriage is the way to create as many potential saints, prophets and Gods as possible. Indeed, plural marriage has to be seen as a Mormon obligation: If divinity tastes so good, then why keep all the goodness to oneself? Spread the big love. It makes perfect sense (at least for heterosexual men).

In his quasi-prophetic manner, Bloom thought the future belonged to Mormonism, concluding, "I cheerfully prophesy that some day, not too far in the twenty-first century, the Mormons will have enough political and financial power to sanction polygamy again. Without it, in some form or other, the complete vision of Joseph Smith never can be fulfilled."

It makes little sense to say that Mormonism is *not* Christian. It's right there in the Mormon articles of faith that were adapted from Smith's famous Wentworth Letter from 1842. Article 1 reads, "We believe in God, the Eternal Father, and in his Son, Jesus Christ, and in the Holy Ghost." But, as Bloom makes compellingly clear, Mormonism is not *just* Christian. The new revelation given to Joseph Smith in his visions and the annual visits of the angel Moroni from 1820 onward is a new gospel for the new world. Mormonism is an American religion, which beautifully, if fallaciously, understands the native inhabitants of the New World as ancient descendants of inhabitants of the Old World, the scattered tribes of Israel. Article 10 reads, "We believe in the literal gathering of Israel and the restoration of the ten tribes; that Zion (the New Jerusalem) will be built upon the American continent." I don't know whether Prime Minister Benjamin Netanyahu has read this article of faith, but it might have some specific consequences for American foreign policy should his close friend and former colleague at the Boston Consulting Group, Mitt Romney, be elected.

Mormonism is properly and powerfully *post*-Christian, just as Islam is post-Christian. Where Islam, which also has a prophet, claims the transcendence of God, Mormonism makes God radically immanent. Where Islam unifies all creatures under one mighty God to whom we must submit, Mormonism pluralizes divinity, making it an immanent, corporeal matter and making God a more fragile, hemmed-in and finite being. Both Islam and Mormonism have a complex relation to the practice of plural marriage.

Yet unlike Islam, for whom Muhammad is the last prophet, Mormonism allows for continuing revelation. In a way, it is very democratic, very American. Article 9 reads, "We believe all that God has revealed, all that He does now reveal, and we believe that He will yet reveal many great and important things pertaining to the Kingdom of God." In principle, any male saint can add to the stock and neverending story of revelation and thereby become exalted. From the standpoint of Christianity, both Islam and Mormonism are heresies and—if one is genuine about one's theology, and religion is not reduced to a set of banal moral platitudes—should be treated as such.

Like Bloom, I see Joseph Smith's apostasy as strong poetry, a gloriously presumptive and delusional creation from the same climate as Whitman's, if not enjoying quite the same air quality. Perhaps Mormonism is not so far from Romanticism after all. To claim that it is simply Christian is to fail to grasp its theological, poetic and political audacity. It is much more than mere Christianity. Why are Mormons so keen to conceal their pearl of the greatest price? Why is no one talking about it? In the context of you-know-who's presidential bid, people appear to be endlessly talking about Mormonism, but its true theological challenge is entirely absent from the discussion.

7
The Freedom of Faith—A Christmas Sermon

December 23, 2012

In an essay in *The New York Times* Sunday Book Review this week the writer Paul Elie asks the intriguing question Has fiction lost its faith?

As we are gathered here today, let us consider one of the most oddly faithful of all fiction writers, Fyodor Dostoevsky. More specifically, I'd like focus on what some consider to be the key moment in his greatest novel—arguably one of the greatest novels of all time—*The Brothers Karamazov*. (Elie himself notes the 1880 masterpiece as an example of the truly faith-engaged fiction of yore.) I speak in particular of the "Grand Inquisitor" scene, a sort of fiction within a fiction that draws on something powerful from the New Testament—Jesus's refusal of Satan's three temptations—and in doing so digs at the meaning of faith, freedom, happiness and the diabolic satisfaction of our desires.

First, a little biblical background.

Scene 1—In Which Christ Is Sorely Tempted by Satan

After fasting for forty days and forty nights in the desert, Jesus is understandably a little hungry. Satan appears and tempts him. The temptation takes the form of three questions. The first involves food. The Devil says, and I paraphrase, "If you are, as you say, the son of God, then turn these stones in the parched and barren wilderness into loaves of bread. Do this, not so much to feed yourself, starved as you are, as to feed those that might follow you, O Son of God. Turn these stones into loaves and people will follow you like sheep ever after. Perform this miracle and people will happily become your slaves."

Jesus replies, "Not on bread alone shall man live, but on every word proceeding through the mouth of God." In other words: "Eat the bread of heaven." Jesus refuses to perform the miracle that he could easily carry out—he is, after all, God. In the name of what does he refuse? We will get to that.

Next Jesus is brought up to the roof of the temple in Jerusalem. Satan invites him to throw himself down. For if he is the son of God, then the armies of angels at his command will save him from smashing his feet against the rocks below. Such a party trick, performed in the crowded hubbub of the holy city, would appear to all to be an awesome mystery and would incite the loyal to devotion. Mystery, by definition, cannot be understood. But Jesus flatly refuses the temptation, saying, "Thou shalt not overtempt the God of thee."

The third temptation raises the stakes even higher. Satan takes Jesus to an exceedingly high mountain and shows him all the kingdoms of the inhabited earth. He says to him, "To thee I will give authority and the glory of them, for such is my power and in my power to give. But if you will worship me, then I will give all the power and the glory to you." Jesus's reply is just two words in New Testament Greek: "Go, Satan!"

With these words, the Devil evaporates like dew under a desert sun.

Scene 2—In Which Christ Denies Authority and Affirms the Freedom of Faith

In refusing these three temptations Jesus is denying three potent forces: miracle, mystery and authority. Of course, the three forces are interlinked: the simplest way to get people to follow a leader is by the miraculous guarantee of bread, namely endless economic abundance and wealth. It is the mystery of authority that confirms our trust in it, in an invisible hand or mysterious market forces that tend benevolently to human well-being.

What Satan promises Jesus in the last temptation is complete political authority, the dream of a universal state in which one no longer has to render to God what is God's and to Caesar what is Caesar's. Temporal and eternal power can be unified under one catholic theological and political authority with the avowed aim of assuring universal happiness, harmony and unity.

It sounds great, doesn't it? So why does Jesus refuse Satan's temptations? In John 8, when Jesus is trying to persuade the scribes and Pharisees of his divinity—which proves somewhat difficult—he says that if they have faith in him, their faith will be faith in the truth, and this truth shall make them free, or, better translated, the truth will free (*eleutherosei*). The first thing that leaps to our attention in this passage is the proximity of faith and truth. We see that truth does not consist of the empirical truths of natural science or the propositional truths of logic. Truth here is a kind of *troth,* a loyalty or fidelity to that to which one is betrothed, as in the act of love. The second thing that we notice is the idea that truth, understood as the truth of faith, will free.

A question arises: What is meant by freedom here, and is it in the name of that freedom that Jesus refuses Satan's temptations? Such is the supremely tempting argument of the Grand Inquisitor at the heart of *The Brothers Karamazov*. Truth to tell, it appears to be a rather strange argument, placed as it is in the mouth of the avowed sensualist for whom everything is permitted: Ivan Karamazov. As his younger brother, Alyosha (the purported hero of the book), points out, the argument is apparently in praise of Jesus and not in blame of him.

Scene 3—Be Happy! Why Jesus Must Burn

Ivan has written a prose poem, set in the sixteenth century in Seville, Spain, during the most terrible time of the Inquisition, when heretics were being burnt alive willy-nilly like firebugs. In the poem, after a particularly magnificent auto-da-fé—when almost a hundred heretics were burnt by the Grand Inquisitor, the eminent cardinal, in the presence of the king, the court and its charming ladies—Christ suddenly appears and is recognized at once. People weep for joy, children throw flowers at his feet and a large crowd gathers outside the cathedral. At that moment, the Grand Inquisitor passes by the cathedral and grasps what is happening. His face darkens. Such is his power and the fear he inspires that the crowd falls silent and parts for him. He orders Jesus arrested and thrown into prison.

Later, the Grand Inquisitor silently watches Jesus in his cell for a long time. Face-to-face, they retain eye contact. Neither of them flinches. Eventually the cardinal says, "Tomorrow, I shall condemn thee at the stake as the worst of heretics. And the people who today kissed Thy feet tomorrow at the faintest sign from me will rush to heap up the embers of Thy fire. Knowest Thou that? Yes, maybe Thou knowest it." He adds, "Why, then, art Thou come to hinder us?" Jesus says nothing.

The Grand Inquisitor's final question appears paradoxical: How might the reappearance of Jesus interfere with the functioning of the most holy Catholic Church? Does the Church not bear Christ's name? The answer is fascinating. For the Grand Inquisitor, what Jesus brought into the world was freedom, specifically the freedom of faith: the truth that will free. And this is where we perhaps begin to sympathize with the Grand Inquisitor. He says that for fifteen hundred years Christians have been wrestling with this freedom. The Grand Inquisitor too, when younger, went into the desert, lived on roots and locusts, and tried to attain the perfect freedom espoused by Jesus. "But now it is ended and over for good," he says. "After fifteen centuries of struggle, the Church has at last vanquished freedom, and has done so to make men happy."

Scene 4—Obedience or Happiness?

What is it that makes human beings happy? In a word, bread. And here we return to Jesus's answers to Satan's desert temptations. In refusing to transform the stones into loaves, Jesus rejected bread for the sake of freedom, for the bread of heaven. Jesus refuses miracle, mystery and authority in the name of a radical freedom of conscience. The problem is that this freedom places an excessive burden on human beings. It is too demanding; infinitely demanding, one might say. As Father Mapple, the preacher in the whaleboat pulpit early in Melville's *Moby-Dick*, says (I paraphrase), "God's command is a hard command. In order to obey it, we must disobey ourselves." If the truth shall set you free, then it is a difficult freedom.

The hardness of God's command, its infinitely demanding character, is the reason why, for the Grand Inquisitor, "Man is tormented by no greater anxiety than to find someone quickly to whom he can hand over that gift of freedom with which the miserable creature is born." Give people the miracle of bread, and they will worship you. Remove their freedom with submission to a mystery that passeth all understanding, and they will obey your authority. They will be happy. Lord knows, they may even believe themselves to be free in such happiness.

Freedom as expressed here is not the rigorous freedom of faith but the multiplication of desires whose rapid satisfaction equals happiness. Freedom is debased and governed by a completely instrumental means-end rationality. Yet, to what does it lead? In the rich, it leads to the isolation of hard hedonism and spiritual suicide. In the poor, it leads to a grotesque and murderous envy, a desire to be like the rich. And—as the hypocritical pièce de résistance—both rich and poor are in the grip of an ideology that claims that human beings are becoming more and more globalized and interconnected and thereby united into a virtual world community that overcomes distance. But we are not.

Scene 5—O Lord: The Church Is in League with the Devil

Back in the prison cell with the ever-silent Jesus, the Grand Inquisitor acknowledges that because of the excessive burden of freedom of conscience, "We have corrected Thy work and founded it on miracle, mystery and authority." This is why the Grand Inquisitor says, "Why hast Thou come to hinder us?"

Then comes the truly revelatory moment in the Grand Inquisitor's monologue, which Jesus knows already (obviously, because he is God). Knowing that he knows, the cardinal says, "Perhaps it is Thy will to hear it from my lips. Listen, then. We are not working with Thee, but with him—that is our mystery." The Church is league with the Devil. It sits astride the Beast and raises aloft the cup marked "Mystery." The Grand Inquisitor is diabolical. This explains why he is so fascinated with the temptations that Jesus faced in the desert. The Church has been seduced by those temptations in Jesus's name.

The paradox is that the Church accepted those temptations in the hope of finding—as the Grand Inquisitor elegantly puts it—"some means of uniting all in one unanimous and harmonious ant-heap." The dream of a universal church, or a universal state, or the unity of all nations, or a cosmopolitan world order founded on perpetual peace, or whatever, is Satan's most persuasive and dangerous temptation. The freedom proclaimed by Jesus is too demanding and makes people unhappy. We prefer a demonic happiness to an unendurable freedom. All that human beings want is to be saved from the great anxiety and terrible agony they endure at present in making free decisions for themselves.

Scene 6—The Kiss and the Curse

And so, all will be happy, except those, like the Grand Inquisitor, who guard the mystery and know the secret. They will be unhappy. But the price is worth paying. The true Christians, by contrast, see themselves as the elect, the twelve thousand from each of the twelve tribes who will be the company of saints in the millennium that follows Christ's Second Coming. This is why the Grand Inquisitor says, "I turned back and joined the ranks of those who have corrected Thy work. I left the proud and went back to the humble, for the happiness of the humble." This is why Christ hinders the work of the Church and why he must burn as a heretic.

At this point, the Grand Inquisitor stops speaking. Silence descends. The prisoner Jesus continues to look gently into the old cardinal's face, who longs for him to say something, no matter how terrible. Jesus rises, approaches the old man and softly kisses his bloodless lips. The Grand Inquisitor shudders, but the kiss still glows in his heart. He stands and heads for the door, saying to Jesus, "Go, and come no more . . . Come not at all . . . never, never!"

Scene 7—Demonic Happiness or Unbearable Freedom?

Back with the two brothers: Ivan immediately disavows the poem as senseless and naive. But Alyosha upbraids Ivan, claiming he is an atheist and saying, "How will you live and how will you love with such a hell in your heart?" As Father Zossima says, "What is hell? I maintain that it is the incapacity to love." The recollections and exhortations of Father Zossima are intended as a refutation of Ivan's in the following chapters of the book. Here the scene ends with Alyosha softly kissing Ivan on the lips, an act that the latter objects to as plagiarism.

Dostoevsky in no way wants to defend the position that Ivan Karamazov outlines in his poem. But Dostoevsky's great virtue as a writer is to be utterly convincing in outlining what he doesn't believe and deeply unconvincing in defending what he wants to believe. As Blake said of *Paradise Lost*, Satan gets all the best lines. The story of the Grand Inquisitor places a stark choice in front of us: demonic happiness or unbearable freedom?

And this choice conceals another, deeper one: truth or falsehood? The truth that sets free does not, as we saw, give freedom of inclination and freedom from passing desire. It is the freedom of faith. It is the acceptance—submission, even— to a demand that both places a perhaps intolerable burden on the self and energizes a movement of subjective conversion, a demand that we begin again. In disobeying ourselves and obeying this hard command, we may put on new selves. Faith hopes for grace.

Scene 8—In Which Doubt and Faith Unite

To be clear, such an experience of faith is not certainty but is gained only by going into the proverbial desert and undergoing diabolical temptation and radical doubt. On this view, doubt is not the enemy of faith. On the contrary, certainty is. If faith becomes certainty, then we have become seduced by the temptations of miracle, mystery and authority. We have become diabolical. There are no guarantees in faith. It is defined by an essential insecurity, tempered by doubt and defined by a radical experience of freedom.

Choosing uncertain faith is to take a noble and, indeed, God-like position. It is also what Jesus demands of us elsewhere in his teaching, in the Sermon on the Mount, when he says, "Love your enemies, bless them that curse you, do good to them that hate you, and pray for them which despitefully use you or persecute you." If that wasn't tough enough, Jesus adds, "Be ye therefore perfect, even as your father which is in heaven is perfect." This is a sublime demand. It is a glorious demand. But it is, finally, a ridiculous demand. Inhuman, even. It is the demand to become perfect, God-like. Easy for Jesus to say, for he was God. But more difficult for us.

Scene 9—In Which the Grand Inquisitor Is, Finally, Defended

So what about us human beings, feeble, imperfect, self-deceived—the weakest reeds in nature? Does not Jesus's insistence on the rigor and purity of faith seem, if not like pride, then at least like haughtiness? The Grand Inquisitor, and the institution of the Church that he represents, accepted Satan's temptations not out of malice but out of a genuine love for humanity. The choice was based on the recognition of our flawed imperfection and our need to be happy. We perhaps deserve happiness.

If the cost of the pure rigor of true faith is the salvation of the happy few, then the rest of us, in our millions and billions, are condemned to a life that is a kind of mockery. The seemingly perverse outcome of Dostoevsky's parable is that perhaps the Grand Inquisitor is morally justified in choosing a lie over the truth.

The Grand Inquisitor's dilemma is, finally, tragic: he knows that the truth which sets us free is too demanding for us, and that the lie that grants happiness permits the greatest good to the greatest number. But he also knows that happiness is a deception that leads ineluctably to our damnation. Is the Grand Inquisitor's lie not a noble one?

Scene 10—In Which the Author Expresses Doubt

To be perfectly (or imperfectly) honest, I don't know the answer to the question. Which should we choose: diabolical happiness or unendurable freedom? Perhaps we should spend days and nights fasting in the desert and see what we might do. Admittedly, fasting is difficult to sustain during the holiday period.

Happy holidays!

8

The Rigor of Love

August 8, 2010

Can the experience of faith be shared by those unable to believe in the existence of a transcendent God? Might there be a faith of the faithless?

For a non-Christian such as myself, but one out of sympathy with the triumphal evangelical atheism of the age, the core commandment of Christian faith has always been a source of fascinated perplexity. What is the status and force of that deceptively simple five-word command "You shall love your neighbor"? With Gary Gutting's wise counsel on the relation between philosophy and faith still ringing in our ears, I'd like to explore the possible meaning of these words through a reflection on a hugely important and influential philosopher not yet even mentioned so far in The Stone: Søren Kierkegaard (1813–55).

In the conclusion to *Works of Love* (1847)—which some consider the central work of Kierkegaard's extensive and often pseudonymous authorship—he ponders the nature of the commandment of love that he has been wrestling with throughout the book. He stresses the strenuousness and, in the word most repeated in his pages, the *rigor* of love. Christian love is not, as many nonbelievers contend, some sort of "coddling love," which spares believers any particular effort. Such love can be characterized as "pleasant days or delightful days without self-made cares." This easy and fanciful idea of love reduces Christianity to "a second childhood" and renders faith infantile.

Kierkegaard introduces instead the concept of the "Christian like-for-like," which is the central and decisive category of *Works of Love*. The Christian like-for-like is introduced by distinguishing it from what Kierkegaard calls the "Jewish like-for-like," by which he means "an eye for an eye, a tooth for a tooth": a conception of obligation based on the equality and reciprocity of self and other. Although, as a cursory reading of Franz Rosenzweig's *The Star of Redemption*—one of the great works of German-Jewish thought—could easily show, this is a stereotypical and limited picture of Judaism, Kierkegaard's point is that Christian love cannot be reduced to what he calls the "worldly" conception of love, where you do unto others what others do unto you and no more. The Christian like-for-like brackets out the question of what others may owe to others and instead "makes every relationship to other human beings into a God-relationship."

This move coincides with a shift from the external to the inward. Although the Christian, for Kierkegaard, "must remain in the world and the relationships of earthly life allotted to him," the Christian views those relationships from the standpoint of inwardness as mediated through the relationship to God. As Kierkegaard puts it emphatically in Part 1 of *Works of Love:*

> Worldly wisdom thinks that love is a relationship between man and man. Christianity teaches that love is a relationship between: man-God-man, that is, that God is the middle term.

The rigor of Christianity is a conception of love based on radical inequality: on the absolute difference between the human and the divine. This is how Kierkegaard interprets Jesus's words from the Sermon on the Mount, "Why do you see the speck that is in your brother's eye, but do not notice the log that is in your own eye?"(Matthew 7:3). The log in my own eye does not permit me to *judge* the speck in the other's. Rather, I should abstain from any judgment of what others might or might not do. To judge others is to view matters from the standpoint of externality rather than from the standpoint of inwardness. It is arrogance and impertinence. What others owe to me is none of my business.

The rigor of this approach is why it is very hard to be Christian. And maybe there are not as many true Christians around as one might have thought. Kierkegaard writes, "Christianly understood, you have absolutely nothing to do with what others do to you. . . . Essentially, you have only to do with yourself before God." Once again, the move to inwardness does not turn human beings away from the world; it is, rather, "a new version of what other men call reality." It *is* reality.

Kierkegaard's writing is specifically addressed to the second person singular, *you.* He tells the story from the Gospels (versions appear in Matthew and Luke) of the Roman centurion in Capernaum who approached Jesus and asked him to cure his boy (or servant; the sense is ambiguous) who was "sick with the palsy, grievously tormented"(Matthew 8:6). After Jesus said that he would visit the boy, the centurion confessed that, as a representative of the occupying imperial authority with soldiers under his command, he did not feel worthy to have Jesus enter his house. When Jesus heard this, he declared that he had not experienced a person of such great faith in the whole of Israel. He added, and this is the line that interests Kierkegaard, "Be it done for you, as you believed."

This story reveals the essential insecurity of faith. Kierkegaard writes that it does not belong to Christian doctrine to vouchsafe that you—"precisely *you*," as he emphasizes—have faith. If someone were to say, "It is absolutely certain that I have faith because I have been baptized in the church and follow its rituals and ordinances," Kierkegaard would reply, "Be it done for you, as you believed." The point of the story is that the centurion believed. As Kierkegaard writes, "In his faith, *the* Gospel is first *a* gospel." The New Testament Greek for "gospel" is *euaggelion,* which can mean good tidings but can also be thought of as the act of proclamation or pledging. On this view, faith is a proclamation or pledge that brings the inward subject of faith into being over against an external everydayness. Such a proclamation is as true for the non-Christian as for the Christian. Indeed, it is arguably more true for non-Christians because their faith is not supported by the supposed guarantee of baptism, creedal dogma, regular church attendance or some notion that virtue will be rewarded with happiness, if not here on earth, then in the afterlife. Thus, paradoxically, non-Christian faith might be said to reveal the true nature of the faith that Christ sought to proclaim. Even—especially—those who are denominationally faithless can have an experience of faith. If faith needs to be underpinned by some sort of doctrinal security, inwardness becomes externalized and the strenuous rigor of faith evaporates.

What sort of certainty, then, is the experience of faith? Kierkegaard writes, and again the second person singular direction of his address should be noted: "It is eternally certain that it will be done for you as you believe, but the certainty of faith, or the certainty that *you, you in particular,* believe, you must win at every moment with God's help, consequently not in some external way" (emphasis mine).

Kierkegaard insists—and one feels here the force of his polemic against the irreligious, essentially secular order of so-called Christendom, in particular against what he saw as the pseudo-Christianity of the Danish National Church—that no pastor or priest has the right to say whether one has faith according to doctrines like baptism. To proclaim faith is to abandon such external or worldly guarantees. Faith has the character of a continuous "striving . . . in which you get occasion to be tried every day." This is why faith, and the commandment of love that it seeks to sustain, is not law. It has no coercive, external force. As Rosenzweig writes, "The commandment of love can only proceed from the mouth of the lover." He contrasts this with law, "which reckons with times, with a future, with duration." The commandment of love "knows only the moment; it awaits the result in the very moment of its promulgation." The commandment of love is mild and merciful, but, as Kierkegaard insists, "there is rigor in it." We might say love is that disciplined act of absolute spiritual daring that eviscerates the old self of externality so something new and inward can come into being.

As Kierkegaard puts in earlier in *Works of Love*, citing Paul, "Owe no one anything, except to love one another" (Romans 13:8). It sounds simple. But what is implicit in this minimal-sounding command is a conception of love as an experience of infinite debt—a debt that it is impossible to repay: "When a man is gripped by love, he feels that this is like being in infinite debt." To be is to be in debt—I owe, therefore I am.

If sin is the theological name for the essential ontological indebtedness of the self, then love is the experience of a countermovement to sin that is oriented to a demand that exceeds the capacity or ability of the self. Love is shaped in relation to what, in my parlance, can be called an infinite demand. Kierkegaard writes, and the double emphasis on "moment" that

finds an echo in Rosenzweig should be noted, "God's relationship to a human being is the infinitizing at every moment of
that which at every moment is in a man." When the self is
withdrawn into inwardness and solitude ("If you have never
been solitary, you have never discovered that God exists," Kierkegaard writes), its every word and action resounds through
the infinite demand of God.

At this point, in the penultimate paragraph of *Works of
Love*, Kierkegaard shifts to auditory imagery. God is a vast echo
chamber where each sound, "the slightest sound," is duplicated
and and echoes loudly in the subject's ears. God is nothing more
than the name for the repetition of each word that the subject
utters. But it is a repetition that resounds with "the intensifica-
tion of infinity." In what Kierkegaard calls the "urban confusion"
of external life, it is nigh impossible to hear this repetition of
the infinite demand. This is why the bracketing out of externality is essential: "Externality is too dense a body for resonance,
and the sensual ear is too hard-of-hearing to catch the eternal's
repetition." We need to cultivate the inner or inward ear that
infinitizes the words and actions of the self. As Kierkegaard
makes clear, what he is counseling is not "to sit in the anxiety
of death, day in and day out, listening for the repetition of the
eternal." What he calls for instead is a rigorous and activist
conception of faith that proclaims itself into being at each instant
without guarantee or security and that abides with the infinite
demand of love.

Faith is not a like-for-like relationship of equals but the
asymmetry of the like-to-unlike. It is a subjective strength that
finds its power to act only through an admission of weakness.
Faith is an enactment of the self in relation to an infinite demand
that both exceeds an individual's power and requires all of it.
Such an experience of faith is not only shared by those who are
faithless from a creedal or denominational perspective but

can—in my view—be had by them in an exemplary manner. Like the Roman centurion of whom Kierkegaard writes, it is perhaps the faithless who can best sustain the rigor of faith without requiring security, guarantees and rewards: "Be it done for you, as you believed."

9
Coin of Praise

August 30, 2009

It is a peculiar fact that the severe economic turmoil of the past year has for the most part not led people to ask the most fundamental question about the root of all this angst: What is money?

Money is, of course, many things: the coins and notes rattling and rustling in our pockets, as well as the piles of real and virtual stuff lying in banks, and the smart money that tends toward increasing immateriality as it is shuffled electronically along the vectors of the financial networks.

That list might serve as an initial, empirical description, but what does money really mean? What is the idea of money that we hold in our minds as we accept it, exchange it, squander it or save it? The core of money is trust and promise: "I promise to pay the bearer on demand the sum of X" on the British pound; the "In God We Trust" of the U.S. dollar; the BCE-ECB-EZB-EKT-EKP of the European Central Bank that runs like a Franco-Anglo-Germano-Greco-Finnish cipher across the top of every euro note.

In other words, the legitimacy of money is based on a sovereign guarantee that the money is good, that it is not counterfeit. Money has a promissory structure with a strangely circular logic: money promises that the money is good. The acceptance of the promise is the approval of a specific monetary ethos. We all agree that the money is worth—in the best of circumstances—more than the paper on which it is printed. To buy and sell using the U.S. dollar, or any other currency, is to trust that each bill is making a promise that it can keep.

This ethos, this circular money-promising-that-the-money-is-good, is underwritten by sovereign power. It is worth recalling that gold coins called sovereigns were first minted in England under Henry VII in 1489; production continues to this day. It is essential that we believe in this power, that the sovereign power of the bank inspires belief, that the "Fed has cred." Credit can operate only on the basis of credence and credibility, as an act of fidelity and faith (*fides*), of con-fid-ence. As historians of language have shown, there is a strong etymological link between ideas of belief, faith and forms of economic exchange. The goddess Fides (Trust) was sometimes depicted on the verso of Roman coins. *In Fed We Trust,* as the title of David Wessel's book has it.

A theological core of money is based on an act of faith, of belief. One can even speak of a sort of monetary civil religion or currency patriotism. This is particularly evident in attitudes in the United States to the dollar, particularly to the sheer material quality of the bill. It can also be found in the U.K.'s opposition to the euro and to the strange cultural need for money marked with the queen's head and underwritten by the power of the sovereign, who is also—lest one forget—the head of the established church.

Plato defines a simulacrum as something that materializes an absence, an image for something that doesn't exist in reality—for example, the god Poseidon or Bob the Builder. Such is money, in my view. In the absence of any gold standard (but ask yourself, How real is the value of gold? Is it not simply yellowish metal?), money is sustained through an act of faith, belief, promise and trust in sovereign power.

To push this a little further, we might say that in the seemingly godless world of global finance capitalism, money is the only thing in which we really must have faith. Money is the one, true god in which we all believe. It is this faith that we celebrate in our desire for commodities, that we see in the kind of fetishistic control that they seem to have over us. It's not so much that we revere the things that money can buy. Rather, we venerate the money that enables us to buy those things. In the alluring displays of shiny brands that cover the marketplace, it is not so much branded objects that we desire as those objects as incarnations of a quantifiable sum of money.

To wear a brand is to display the money that was able to buy it. With us, it is not so much that the money changers have desecrated the temple; rather, the only temples where we can worship are places where money changes hands in some perverse parody of a religious service. This strange mass is what we celebrate in the cathedral-like malls that litter the land.

It is an understandable misunderstanding of capitalism to declare that it is a materialism that consists of a voracious desire for things. I would argue that we love the money that enables us to buy those things, for it reaffirms our faith and restores the only theological basis we have for our trust in the world. Money is our metaphysics. In that god we trust. And when trust breaks down, as it has done so dramatically in the past year, people experience something close to a crisis of faith.

In response to this crisis, the only political response (by Obama-Geithner-Summers over here and Brown-Merkel-Sarkozy over there) is the attempt to restore faith, to shore up the credit systems by making governments the banks of last resort. Sadly—or happily for the politicians—people have short memories, and their momentary crisis of faith is washed away in the waters of forgetfulness and overcome by a relentless will to believe.

As ever, Shakespeare elucidated this powerfully. In *Timon of Athens,* the protagonist speaks of money, in the form of gold, as "thou visible God / That sold'rest close impossibilities / And makest them kiss!" In other words, there is nothing that money cannot solder together. Another phrase from the same play calls gold "Thou common whore of mankind." Money, we might say, is both the visible God and the common whore.

As a learned philosopher once remarked, money is the pimp between need and object, making available all objects and objectifying all beings, especially human beings. In a society like ours, where money is the one true God, everything is for sale and everyone is a prostitute insofar as value can be ultimately determined in financial terms.

Some readers may object that my approach is overly philosophical and doesn't help if you've lost your house and medical insurance. True enough! But the curious thing about money is that something so real can at the same time be so illusory.

10

Soccer Fandom as a Model for Living

August 15, 2018

The decision was made instantly. My son Edward was in Rome for the second leg of Liverpool's Champions League soccer semifinal on May 2. I was in New York pretending to prepare for a class but really watching the game at home in Brooklyn. We are devoted fans of Liverpool Football Club. We were texting throughout the game. Although Liverpool lost the match with Roma, we won the tie over two legs and reached the Champions League final for the first time in eleven years to face the mighty Real Madrid, which had won the competition the previous two years. On May 26, we had the chance to win the most important soccer club competition in the world. As every fan knows, the top European clubs are much stronger than national teams and arguably much more significant. This was our chance to resume our rightful place among soccer's European royalty and make history.

We had to watch the game together. Where and how? We reviewed the options. The final was in Kiev. We couldn't get tickets. We tried to get into the Anfield Road stadium in

Liverpool to watch it on a huge screen, but seats there were also instantly sold out. The pubs in London were going to be heaving with bodies, and we needed to focus on the game, to concentrate and watch properly. We settled on watching the game in his place in Brixton, South London. His roommates were out at a birthday party, so we would have the place to ourselves. Ideal.

I flew to London and checked into a cheapish local hotel with a nice view of a puddle and an extractor fan. My son and I met in a bar of the Ritzy Cinema and drank a first beer. Three hours until kickoff. The air in London was rich, summery and humid, with a looming threat of serious storms. There was a tingle in the atmosphere. We ate Thai food in the loveliness of Brixton Market surrounded by a hubbub of vape smoke, the pleasant hum of shopping being done and the sound of "Fiery Jack" by The Fall booming out of a tiny vintage clothing store. We stopped at a Sainsbury's supermarket to buy a lot of beer and went to his place and settled in. We were both more than a little nervous.

We lost badly, calamitously, almost comically (although we weren't laughing), with two inexplicable errors from our otherwise remarkably handsome goalkeeper, Loris Karius, and a wondergoal from the Welshman with the topknot, Gareth Bale. But our fans were magnificent and massively outnumbered Madrid supporters. We dominated the stadium with thousands upon thousands of fans decked in red, singing our songs: "Mo Salah, Mo Salah, running down the wing, our Egyptian king." Our fans sang until the bitter end.

And we dominated the game for the twenty-five minutes until Sergio Ramos, the ever-smiling, slightly wacky Real Madrid captain and sometime rapper, wrestled Mohamed Salah to the ground in an armlock and deliberately crushed him with all his body weight. He knew what he was doing: eliminate

Liverpool's best player from the game. Salah left the pitch in
tears with a busted shoulder. It was a totally cynical foul and
should have been punished with a red card or possibly even life
imprisonment. We lost our rhythm, our spirit, our psychical
strength, and never really regained it. Real Madrid took control
of the midfield through the powerful coupling of Luka Modrić
and Toni Kroos, and we slipped back, deeper and deeper, inviting disaster. And disaster happened.

Liverpool fans have rightly hated the Rupert Murdoch–
owned *Sun* newspaper since its wildly erroneous and malevolent
reporting of the Hillsborough disaster in 1989, when ninety-six
Liverpool fans were crushed to death because of the negligent
behavior of the South Yorkshire police. Consistent with its
xenophobic support of Thatcher's Tory government, *The Sun*
blamed the fans for their own deaths, calling them "Scum." But
the newspaper is good at headlines. On Sunday, May 27, the
soccer page at the back of it read: "Loris 'N Hardy. Another fine
mess from Karius as Bale cashes in on Mo woe." Not a bad
summary of the game.

It's difficult to describe the feeling after losing a game like
this, in the way we did. A total flatness, a stunned emptiness,
with no desire to speak much. Ed and I sat quietly in his front
room, turned down the volume on the TV and steadily drank
more beer, messaging friends with difficulty and no real interest. Life felt sucked dry. I suggested feebly that we go to the pub,
but he declined, saying he was not feeling up to it. Nor was I,
to tell the truth. At that moment, like a good metaphor, a vast
storm broke over South London, with wild lightning and rivers
of rain in the streets.

What does being a soccer fan teach us about being human?
A lot more than AncestryDNA, as it turns out. Soccer gives us
a lived experience of community with fellow fans. It provides
a history for that experience and a robust feeing of identity,

place and belonging, even when that belonging is virtual, circulating through television screens and across social media networks. Being a Liverpool fan is also about a set of values: solidarity, compassion, internationalism, decency, honor, self-respect and respect for others, even Manchester United fans (well, sometimes).

Soccer is also about the bonds of love, of being together passionately around a wealth of history that is held in common. This history is intensely personal, visceral. My grandmother has a Liverpool Football Club crest on her gravestone. The only thing I could talk about sensibly and rationally with my father until he died was soccer. Eighty percent of my texting and talking with my son is about the team. That's a century and counting of history. And millions upon millions of fans from all across the world have very similar sets of experiences. And these experiences all link together into the vast collective body of emotions and words that constitute the cosmos of fandom. The fans are a living archive, a repository for the meaning and values of a club. Players come and go, so do coaches, but the fans are the existential memory of the team. Without them, the game is nothing. With them, it is more than a game.

Happily, despite all the horrors of the world, human beings are playful creatures who are able to give themselves over to games, engaging in them and watching them. Play is a relief and a release from the pressure of reality, but also a way of engaging that reality, indirectly, lightly, joyfully. Somehow, in play, we are able to give ourselves a little holiday in life that is not simply an escapist distraction but a way of seriously engaging with the ties that bind us together.

Mainly being a fan is about learning to accept failure, loss and huge bewildering disappointment, such as happened on May 26. It is *so* difficult to get to a Champions League final. After all the time and passion that fans invested in watching all the games this season, to lose in the way we did is heartbreaking. Yet, in this loss, the fans are still together, arguably more together than ever. Liverpool's club song is a moving rendition of the maybe cheesy Rodgers and Hammerstein 1945 showtune "You'll Never Walk Alone." In loss, we are still together. I have watched a lot of Liverpool games with my son when we have lost. We lost to Sevilla in the Europa League final in 2016. We lost to Milan in the Champions League final of 2007. We will lose again. The important thing is being together when you lose: soccer can teach the virtues of togetherness and solidarity.

Truth to tell, losing is not the worst thing about football. Every team loses. Has to lose. What kills you as a fan is not the disappointment but the *hope* that comes into the room to tickle your feet. Then you realize that your soles are on fire. Despite loss, hope flickers and burns. Next time, we say. Next time. The problem is, we half-believe when we say it.

The only religious commitment I have is to Liverpool Football Club. I worship the gods, heroes and ancestors of my team, recount the myths we have in common and engage in the often highly elaborate social ritual of watching the team at least once a week, usually twice. But if soccer is a religion, it is polytheistic, with the many local gods of former players and coaches. But other teams have their gods, their ancestors, their myths and legends. Real Madrid fans and even Chelsea fans have their gods. What is so interesting about soccer is that it permits, indeed encourages, powerfully held belief in your team as the best team, as a unique presence, while acknowledging that fans of other teams also worship their gods in their way. It allows a passionately held relativity of belief. Soccer is a little like polytheism in ancient Greece. The Athenians, Spartans and Thebans all had their gods and rituals; those gods were very often linked, but they were distinct and locally situated. Everything goes wrong with religion when a belief in the exclusivity of your god merges together with a universalistic dogma that one's god is the only true god. In my humble opinion, polytheism is vastly preferable to monotheism.

Speaking of local gods, before saying good-bye to my son and going back to Heathrow for one more experience of the singular melancholy of air travel with inevitable delays due to further storms, we went to see the David Bowie mural outside Brixton subway station. Bowie spent the first six years of his life close to that spot. We talked and took photos of each other, and I examined the multiple inscriptions on the mural. Somehow, at that moment, for reasons that I find difficult to piece together, life made sense.

Being human is being a fan. But being a fan does not entail fanaticism.

Postscript, June 2019: Liverpool reached the final of the Champions League for a second successive season after an extraordinary campaign that involved defeating FC Barcelona in a truly heroic match, where, on May 7, a 3–0 deficit in the first leg at the Camp Nou was overturned by a 4–0 victory at Anfield. The final took place on June 1 in Madrid. Edward and I moved heaven and earth to be there. He drove down all the way from London, which took days, and I flew from Norway, which cost a lot of euros. We met in Madrid on the morning of the game. I tried every possible avenue but couldn't get hold of tickets, so after a long, wonderful day in the Liverpool fan zone, we found our way to a packed bar close to the Plaza Mayor. This time, we won. Our sixth victory. It is impossible to describe the intensity and the joy of that evening in Madrid. True, there is a virtue in learning from defeat, but victory feels nice too.

What Are Philosophers For?

11

What Is a Philosopher?

May 16, 2010

There are as many definitions of philosophy as there are philosophers—perhaps there are even more. After three millennia of philosophical activity and disagreement, it is unlikely that we'll reach consensus, and I certainly don't want to add more hot air to the volcanic cloud of unknowing. What I'd like to do in the opening column in this new venture—The Stone—is to kick things off by asking a slightly different question: What is a philosopher?

As Alfred North Whitehead said, philosophy is a series of footnotes to Plato. Let me risk adding a footnote by looking at Plato's provocative definition of the philosopher that appears in the middle of the *Theaetetus*, in a passage that some scholars consider a "digression." Far from being a footnote to a digression, this moment in Plato tells us something hugely important about what a philosopher is and what philosophy does.

Socrates tells the story of Thales, who was by some accounts the first philosopher. He was looking so intently at the stars that he fell into a well. Some witty Thracian servant girl is said to have made a joke at Thales's expense—that in his eagerness to know what went on in the sky he was unaware of the things in front of him and at his feet. Socrates adds, in Seth Benardete's translation, "The same jest suffices for all those who engage in philosophy."

What is a philosopher, then? The answer is clear: a laughingstock, an absentminded buffoon, the butt of countless jokes from Aristophanes's *The Clouds* to Mel Brooks's *History of the World: Part I.* Whenever the philosopher is compelled to talk about the things at his feet, he gives not only the Thracian girl but the rest of the crowd a belly laugh. The philosopher's clumsiness in worldly affairs makes him appear stupid or at least "gives the impression of plain silliness." We are left with a rather Monty Pythonesque definition of the philosopher: the one who is silly.

But as always with Plato, things are not necessarily as they first appear, and Socrates is the greatest of ironists. First, we should recall that Thales believed that water was the universal substance out of which all things were composed. Water was Thales's philosopher's stone, as it were. Therefore, by falling into a well, he inadvertently pressed his basic philosophical claim.

There is a deeper and more troubling layer of irony here, however, that I would like to peel off more slowly. Socrates introduces the digression by making a distinction between the philosopher and the lawyer, or what Benardete nicely renders as the "pettifogger." The lawyer is compelled to present a case in court, and time is of the essence. In Greek legal proceedings, a strictly limited amount of time was allotted for the presentation of cases. Time was measured with a water clock, or klepsydra, which literally steals time, as in the Greek *kleptes,* a thief or embezzler. The pettifogger, the jury and, by implication, the whole society live with the constant pressure of time. The water of time's flow is constantly threatening to drown them.

By contrast, we might say, the philosopher is the person who has time or who takes time. Theodorus, Socrates's interlocutor, introduces the digression with the words, "Aren't we at leisure, Socrates?" The latter's response is interesting. He says, "It appears we are." As we know, in philosophy appearances can be deceptive. But the basic contrast here is that between the lawyer, who has no time, or for whom time is money, and the philosopher, who takes time. The freedom of the philosopher consists in either moving freely from topic to topic or simply spending years returning to the same topic out of perplexity, fascination and curiosity.

Pushing this a little further, we might say that to philosophize is to take your time, even when you have no time, when time is constantly pressing at your back. The busy readers of *The New York Times* will doubtless understand this sentiment. It is our hope that some of them will make the time to read The Stone. As Wittgenstein says, "This is how philosophers should salute each other: 'Take your time.' " Indeed, it might tell you something about the nature of philosophical dialogue to confess that my attention was recently drawn to this passage from *Theaetetus* in leisurely discussions with a doctoral student at the New School, Charles Snyder.

Socrates says that those in the constant press of business, like lawyers, policymakers, mortgage brokers and hedge fund managers, become "bent and stunted" and are compelled "to do crooked things." The pettifogger is undoubtedly successful, wealthy and extraordinarily honey-tongued, but, Socrates adds, "small in his soul and shrewd and a shyster." The philosopher, by contrast, is *free* by virtue of otherworldliness, by the capacity to fall into wells and appear silly.

Socrates adds that the philosopher neither sees nor hears the so-called unwritten laws of the city—that is, the mores and conventions that govern public life. The philosopher shows no

respect for rank and inherited privilege and is unaware of anyone's high or low birth. Nor does it occur to the philosopher to
join a political club or a private party. As Socrates concludes,
the philosopher's body alone dwells within the city's walls. In
thought, the philosopher is elsewhere.

This sounds dreamy, but it isn't. Philosophy should come
with the kind of health warning one finds on packs of European cigarettes: PHILOSOPHY KILLS. Here we approach the deep
irony of Plato's words. Plato's dialogues were written after
Socrates's death. Socrates was charged with displaying impiety
toward the gods of the city and with corrupting the youth of
Athens. He was obliged to speak in court in defense of these
charges, to speak against the water clock, that thief of time. He
ran out of time and suffered the consequence: he was condemned to death and forced to take his own life.

A couple of generations later, during the uprisings against
Macedonian rule that followed the death of Alexander the Great
in 323 BCE, Alexander's former tutor, Aristotle, escaped Athens,
saying, "I will not allow the Athenians to sin twice against
philosophy." From the ancient Greeks to Giordano Bruno,
Spinoza, Hume, and right up to the shameful lawsuit that pre-
vented Bertrand Russell from teaching at the City College of
New York in 1940 on the charge of sexual immorality and atheism, philosophy has repeatedly and persistently been identified
with blasphemy against the gods, whichever gods they might
be. Nothing is more common in the history of philosophy than
the accusation of impiety. Because of their laughable otherworldliness and lack of respect for social convention, rank and
privilege, philosophers refuse to honor the old gods, and this
makes them politically suspicious, even dangerous. Might such
dismal things still happen in our happily enlightened age? That
depends on where one casts one's eyes and how closely one
looks.

Perhaps the last laugh is with the philosopher. Although the philosopher will always look ridiculous in the eyes of pettifoggers and those obsessed with maintaining the status quo, the opposite happens when the non-philosopher is obliged to give an account of justice in itself or happiness and misery in general. Far from being eloquent, Socrates insists, the pettifogger is "perplexed and stutters."

One might object that ridiculing someone's stammer isn't a very nice thing to do. Benardete rightly points out that Socrates assigns every kind of virtue to philosophers apart from moderation. Nurtured in freedom and taking their time, there is something dreadfully uncanny about philosophers, something either monstrous or godlike, or, indeed, both at once. This is why many sensible people continue to think the Athenians had a point in condemning Socrates to death. I leave it for you to decide. I couldn't possibly judge.

12

When Socrates Met Phaedrus
Eros in Philosophy

November 3, 2013

Crazy Hot

Let me set the scene. It's hot. It's really hot. It's the middle of the Greek summer. Socrates is in Athens, where he bumps into an acquaintance called Phaedrus. They say hi. They begin to talk.

Phaedrus is excited. He just heard what he thinks is an amazing speech on love—eros—by the orator Lysias. For the ancient Greeks, eros denoted both sexual pleasure and a god. That is, love had both physical and metaphysical aspects.

Socrates persuades Phaedrus to read him the speech (he has a copy hidden under his cloak). After a long morning listening to speeches, Phaedrus is eager to stretch his legs, and Socrates agrees to accompany him on a stroll out of the city. This is only time in all the Platonic dialogues that Socrates leaves the city of Athens. He is no nature boy. Trees have nothing to teach him.

Indeed, the climate influences this dialogue more than any other text by Plato that I know. Such is the heat of eros described by Sappho that

Sweat pours down me, I shake
all over, I go pale as green
grass. I'm that close to being dead

As I said, it's hot.

The two men walk some distance along the Illisos River. They are both barefoot and walk in the water. Sweat pours down their faces. They decide to sit by the banks of the river in the shade of a broad-leaved plane tree—in Greek, a *platanos*. A Plato-tree. It is hardly mere accident that the shade providing the shelter for the dialogue is broad-shouldered Plato—from *platus*, meaning broad—the tree in which cicadas sing.

Socrates tells a story about the cicadas. Because they are so enthused by the Muses, cicadas sing constantly, stopping for neither food nor drink until they die. If cicadas are inspired by the Muses, Socrates suggests, then philosophers should be inspired by cicadas. The difference between philosophers and cicadas is that the former don't sing so beautifully or so constantly . . . although they do get to live longer.

Lounging under a tree by the river, Phaedrus remarks that Socrates appears "to be totally out of place." In leaving the city, Socrates seems to leave himself behind, to become beside himself, to become ecstatic, indeed a little manic. Love, what the Greeks call eros, is, Socrates insists, *manike,* a madness. It's crazy hot.

Eros Is a Force

What is eros? More specifically, what is the eros of philosophy and the philosopher? We commonly understand it to be a force that compels physical love, but we might also speculate whether eros is a force that compels philosophy, a force that is somehow outside the self but toward which the soul can incline itself; whether it is what Socrates calls a god, a force that perhaps even compels the philosopher to leave the cave in Plato's *Republic*. Of course, it is not at all clear how the first prisoner in the cave emancipates himself. He frees the others, but who frees him? The text does not explain. Perhaps eros is the animating and primal force that shapes philosophy and moves the philosopher to break free from the cave and move toward the light.

It is peculiar indeed that the enabling condition for freedom is a force that compels: a compulsion, a necessity. Unconditional freedom appears to be conditioned by what contradicts it. Eros, in making philosophy possible, somehow turns the freedom of the philosopher inside out, back to front. A nice, if totally incidental, peculiarity is that the numerals of the current year, 2013, looked at upside down, backwards and with a slight squint, spell "eros." Perhaps we can only see eros back to front, in the form of indirect communication, as in a dialogue.

Philosophy's Primal Scene

How are we to understand the nature of eros as it appears in Plato's *Phaedrus*? Here we approach the central enigma of the dialogue. For it appears to deal with two distinct topics: eros and rhetoric. My thought is very simple: I will try and show that these twin themes of eros and rhetoric are really one and that they help explain the peculiar form of discourse that Socrates calls philosophy.

For the ancient Greeks, there was a close connection between the passions or emotions, like eros, and rhetoric. We need only recall that Aristotle's discussion of the emotions is in the *Rhetoric*. Emotion was linked to rhetoric for Aristotle because it could influence judgment in the legal, moral or political senses of the word.

In the Athens of Socrates's time, the two groups of people capable of stirring up powerful emotions were the tragic poets and the Sophists. Let's just say that Socrates had issues with both groups. Tragedy, again in Aristotle's sense, stirs up the emotions of pity and fear in a way that leads to their *katharsis,* understood as purgation or, better, purification. The Sophists exploited the link between emotion and rhetoric to teach the art of persuasive speech, which was central to the practice of law and litigation. Classical Athens was a very litigious place but mercifully did not have lawyers. Men (and it was just men) had to defend themselves, and Sophists taught those who could pay a fee how to do so.

Socrates's inability to defend himself in the law court, and the way such an inability is the defining criterion of the philosopher, recurs in dialogue after dialogue, in the *Apology* obviously, but with particular power in the *Theaetetus,* as I tried to suggest in very first column of The Stone in 2010. The philosopher is presented as a kind of madman or fool, like Thales, who falls into ditches because he is contemplating the stars, which makes the Thracian maid laugh. The philosopher is continually contrasted with the pettifogging citizen who speaks in the law court. Where the latter is skilled in speaking in court against the clock—the klepsydra, or water clock, that quite literally steals time—the philosopher has no sense of time and consequently takes his time, but uses it badly. The philosopher's inability to defend himself persuasively in the law court leads directly to his being found guilty and sentenced to execution. That's what happened to Socrates.

Such is the primal scene of philosophy. Socrates is the tragic hero whose death moves the drama off the stage of the Theater of Dionysos on the south slope of the Acropolis into the heart of the city of Athens. To understate matters somewhat, there is no obvious historical alliance between philosophy and democracy. In killing Socrates (and it is highly arguable that this was justified), Athenian democracy stands indicted.

Who Is Phaedrus?

Philosophy's main question, then and now, is, How might there be a true speech that refuses the corrosive effects of bad rhetoric and sophistry? This question brings us back to the *Phaedrus*. The purpose of the dialogue is to arouse an emotion— specifically, a philosophical eros—in the rather unphilosophical Phaedrus.

We have to be honest about Phaedrus. Who is this guy? He is not the kind of feisty, angry and highly intelligent opponent that Socrates finds in Callicles from the *Gorgias* or even Thrasymachus from the *Republic,* let alone the Stranger from the *Sophist,* whose stunning dialectical ability reduces Socrates to silence.

Phaedrus is a simpler soul. He seems to live in order to receive pleasure from listening to speeches. He is like someone nowadays who compulsively watches TED talks. So Socrates gives him that pleasure both to please and to persuade him. Not just once, but twice. Indeed, the sheer length of Socrates's second speech on eros might arouse our suspicion, for we know from elsewhere that Socrates hates long speeches, even when delivered by the most eloquent of speakers. Why is Socrates doing what he hates?

Now, I am not suggesting that Phaedrus is stupid, but he's perhaps not the brightest spark in Athens (admittedly a city with many bright sparks). There appear to be many facts of which he is unaware, and he also keeps forgetting Socrates's argument and needs constant reminders. "So it seemed," he says at one point, "but remind me again how we did it." And this occurs during a discussion of recollection versus reminding. Phaedrus forgets the argument during a discussion of memory. You get the point.

Much of Socrates's rather obvious and extended passages of irony in the dialogue also seem to pass him by. Occasionally, Phaedrus will burst out with something like, "Socrates, you're very good at making up stories from Egypt or wherever else you want." Phaedrus is nice but a bit dim.

Directing the Soul: Bad Rhetoric and Good

Rhetoric is characterized by the Sophist Gorgias as inducing persuasion in the soul of the listener. But Socrates goes further and defines rhetoric as what he calls a *techne psychagogia*, an art of leading or directing the soul, a kind of bewitchment that holds the listener's soul spellbound. The irony here is that it is precisely in these terms that Socrates criticizes the effects of tragic poetry in the *Republic*, which is why poets cannot be admitted into a philosophically well-ordered city.

However, Socrates's speeches in the *Phaedrus* are precisely this kind of bewitching psychagogy. Phaedrus, who loves speeches, is entranced. His soul is successfully conjured by Socrates. The dialogue brings Phaedrus to love philosophy by loving philosophically.

Now, it might appear on a superficial reading that the question of eros disappears in the second half of the *Phaedrus*. But this view is deceptive, for the forensic discussion of Lysias's speech on eros leads to a definition of artful or true speech. The dialogue culminates in a definition of the philosopher as the true lover or lover of truth, by which point Phaedrus is completely persuaded by Socrates.

The intention of the *Phaedrus* is to persuade Phaedrus. Nothing more. The purpose of the dialogue, as Alexander Ne-hemas has convincingly suggested, is to inflame a philosophical eros in Phaedrus that gives him the ability to distinguish bad rhetoric, of the kinds found in Lysias's speech and in Socrates's first speech, from true rhetoric, of the kind found in the second speech and then analyzed in the second half of the dialogue.

What does this suggest about philosophical dialogue? I think it leads us to the view that each dialogue is radically singular, as singular as the proper name of its title. This is why the dialogue is called in Greek *Phaidros*. The dialogue is addressed to a specific and named interlocutor. It meets Phaedrus on his ground (it even walks out with him barefoot into the country-side) and brings him to philosophical eros. It meets him on his own terms, namely in terms of his questionable estimation of the high importance of speeches. It meets him by accepting his preferences, his prejudices, his sense of what matters, and then slowly turning his sophistical delight in speeches into a commitment to philosophy.

The Purpose of Philosophical Dialogue

Philosophy is addressed to a particular and existent other, not the empty personification of some particular virtue or vice (which is arguably the error of the dialogues of later philosophers like Berkeley and Hume, which can appear oddly contrived and wooden). Dialogue is the attempt to persuade that other in terms that the other will understand and accept, whatever it is that the other believes. Otherwise, philosophy is building castles in the air with its concepts, its systems and its bizarre jargon, which go right over the head of someone as unphilosophical as Phaedrus.

In philosophy, we have to meet others on their ground and in their own terms and try and bring them around, slowly, cautiously and with good humor. Socrates does not say how awful he finds Lysias's speech, and he shouldn't. Doing so would mean that the dialogue had failed, and we should note that Platonic dialogues do sometimes fail. For example, Callicles simply refuses to play Socrates's question-and-answer game, and the *Gorgias* ends up as a crazed monologue with Socrates talking to himself. Socrates doesn't always get his way.

But the *Phaedrus* is a success in that Socrates persuades his interlocutor. We might want to say that a philosophical dialogue is more like a case study in psychotherapy, which also sometimes fails. Such case studies might be exemplary and thereby exert a general claim, as the *Phaedrus* unquestionably does, but each dialogue is a singular and highly specific case.

Philosophy as Performance

Socrates specifies the conditions that any rhetoric must meet in order to be a philosophical rhetoric capable of engendering eros. If rhetoric is a kind of psychagogia, or soul-leading, then a philosophical rhetoric must be based on knowledge of the nature of various kinds of souls and which sorts of speeches would appeal to which sorts of souls.

Listen to Socrates's words.

> On meeting someone he will be able to discern what he is like and make clear to himself that the person actually standing in front of him is of just this particular sort of character ... that he must now apply speeches of such-and-such a kind in this particular way in order to secure conviction about such-and-such an issue. When he has learned all

this ... then, and only then, will he have finally
mastered the art well and completely.

This is an exquisite commentary on the very situation in which
Socrates finds himself during the *Phaedrus*. He has to make his
speech address "the person actually standing in front of him."
And "in order to secure conviction," he has to speak to Phaedrus
in terms that Phaedrus will accept. He will have to say the right
thing in the right way at the right time to the person right in
front of him.

The sheer reflexivity of the *Phaedrus* is astonishing. It is
not only a piece of beautiful writing that, in its final scene,
denounces writing. It is also an enactment of the very conditions
of true philosophical rhetoric theorized in the dialogue. It is
the enactment of philosophical theory as a practice of dialogue.
The opposite of a self-contradiction, the *Phaedrus* is a perfor-
mative self-enactment of philosophy.

If eros is a force that shapes the philosopher, then
rhetoric is the art by which the philosopher persuades the non-
philosopher to assume philosophical eros, to incline his or her
soul toward truth. But to do this does not entail abandoning
the art of rhetoric or indeed sophistry, which teaches that art,
although it does so falsely. Philosophy uses true rhetoric against
false rhetoric.

The subject matter of the *Phaedrus* is rhetoric, true
rhetoric. Its intention is to show that veritable eros, as opposed
to the kind of vulgar pederasty that Socrates criticizes and which
was the Athenian specialty of the time. The veritable eros is
both subject *to* true rhetoric and the subject *of* true rhetoric.
Philosophical eros is the effect of rhetoric, of language used
persuasively. Sometimes it succeeds, and sometimes it fails.

13
Cynicism We Can Believe In

March 31, 2009

Some 2,300 years after his death, Diogenes the Cynic dramatically interrupted a recent New York State Senate committee meeting. Wearing a long, white beard and carrying his trademark lamp in broad daylight, the ancient philosopher—who once described himself as "a Socrates gone mad"—claimed to be looking for an honest man in politics. Considering the neverending allegations of financial corruption that flow from the sump of Albany, it's no surprise that he was unsuccessful.

This resurrected Diogenes was Randy Credico, a comedian who says he is considering challenging Senator Charles Schumer in the 2010 Democratic primary. Whatever boost Mr. Credico's prank provides his campaign, it might also cause us to reflect a little on the meaning of cynicism—and how greatly we still need Diogenes.

Cynicism is not at all cynical in the modern sense of the word. It bears no real resemblance to that attitude of negativity and jaded scornfulness that sees the worst of intentions behind the apparent good motives of others.

True cynicism is not a debasement of others but a debasement of oneself—and in that purposeful self-debasement it is a protest against corruption, luxury and insincerity. Diogenes, the story goes, was called a "downright dog," and this so pleased him that the figure of a dog was carved in stone to mark his final resting place. From that epithet, *kunikos* (doglike), cynicism was born.

Diogenes credited his teacher Antisthenes with introducing him to a life of poverty and happiness—of poverty as happiness. The cynic's every word and action was dedicated to the belief that the path to individual freedom required absolute honesty and complete material austerity.

So Diogenes threw away his cup when he saw people drinking from their hands. He lived in a barrel, rolling in it over hot sand in the summer. He inured himself to cold by embracing statues blanketed with snow. He ate raw squid to avoid the trouble of cooking. He mocked the auctioneer while being sold into slavery.

When asked by Lysias the pharmacist if he believed in the gods, he replied, "How can I help believing in them when I see a godforsaken wretch like you?" When he was asked the right time to marry, he said, "For a young man not yet, for an old man never at all." When asked what was the most beautiful thing in the world, Diogenes replied, "Freedom of speech." Sadly, it remains one of the most dangerous.

And when asked where he came from, this native of Sinope, in what is now Turkey, replied that he was a "citizen of the world," or *kosmopolites*. Imagine if today's self-styled cosmopolitans drank water from their hands, hugged statues and lived in barrels! Truth be told, Diogenes's cosmopolitanism was much more of an antipolitical stance than the sort of banal internationalism that people associate with the word today.

Cynicism is basically a moral protest against hypocrisy and cant in politics and excess and thoughtless self-indulgence in the conduct of life. In a world like ours, which is slowly trying to rouse itself from the dogmatic slumbers of boundless self-interest, corruption, lazy cronyism and greed, it is Diogenes's lamp that we need to light our path. Perhaps this recession will make cynics of us all.

14

To Weld, Perchance to Dream

November 14, 2015

It's not often that one finds oneself uniquely qualified to comment on a matter in the popular media, but when Marco Rubio argued at the Republican debate last week that the country needs "more welders and less philosophers," I had my moment. My father was a welder, and I am a philosopher. I actually did have a choice to make some decades ago: to weld or to philosophize?

Rubio got the response he wanted. Philosophiles and sundry humanities defenders gleefully pointed out that what he said was empirically false (philosophy professors apparently earn more than welders). I might also point out Rubio's grammatical error—we need *fewer* philosophers—but that would just be taking the bait, wouldn't it? What kind of useless creature corrects the grammar of powerful men when things need to be joined together with molten metal?

But maybe Rubio has a point. As a friend of mine once elegantly put it: "Philosophy doesn't boil cabbages or skin rabbits." Nor does it spot weld or arc weld. Am I obviously better than my dad was because I get paid to think for a living?

I grew up in and around the factories my dad worked in, and later managed, north of London in the 1960s and 1970s. I started work at the age of fourteen (illegal even then) bending sheet metal on Saturday mornings and making cups of tea for huge, terrifying men who all seemed to have strange naval tattoos on their forearms and hands like bunches of blackened bananas.

Things didn't go well. During what was probably my first hangover after a party (I think I was still fourteen), I lost the top of my right middle finger in the steel rollers of a huge sheet-metal-bending machine. That hurt quite a bit and played havoc with my bass guitar playing.

But I kept working off and on at different factories, and excelled at making tea, cleaning toilets and sweeping up. Sadly, things went from bad to worse. When I was eighteen, during a stint at a pharmaceutical factory that mixed drugs for diabetics, my entire left hand was almost severed after it got trapped in a machine I was cleaning. Someone mistakenly turned on what was euphemistically called the dead man's switch. (Who says there's no irony in the industrial sector?) After two weeks in a hospital, the doctors told me I could keep my hand—it didn't need to be amputated. You can imagine my delight. This injury also played havoc with my guitar playing, so I switched to the synthesizer. Which led to the glittering failure of a musical career.

After nearly losing a digit and a hand in this manner, I thought I probably didn't have much of a future in factories. The thing is, I would have loved to be a welder. Sadly, I was rubbish at work and seemed to possess no practical skills.

I imagine most people think that philosophers are rather effete types, the products of generations of ingrained liberal privilege. I don't want to sound like a working-class hero (what would John Lennon say?), but that is not always the case.

It is useful to recall the oldest story we know about the origins of philosophy. The pre-Socratic thinker Thales falls into a ditch because he's too busy contemplating the heavens and their origins. A Thracian serving girl is said to have laughed heartily at Thales's pratfall.

That's how I like to think about philosophy: it doesn't begin so much in the confined elegance of Oxbridge tutorials as in a ditch with a nasty bruise on one's head and possibly some ligament damage.

You might be wondering why I appear to be so happily shooting myself and my profession in the foot and undermining the lofty business of philosophical contemplation. But it is important to remember where one comes from and the odd choices one had to make.

When I was twenty-two I got lucky and wound up in a university, where I first listened to philosophers teach. I couldn't understand how they had become so smart or how they were able to talk so clearly about matters of such compelling difficulty. I got hooked, and, thanks to the kind of public funding of higher education that has now disappeared from England, I acquired an education and eventually wound up teaching philosophy.

To risk wild understatement, let me point out that philosophers have no observable practical skills and have made no progress on any of the major philosophical questions in nearly three thousand years. This might sound like failure.

But not so fast.

Philosophers don't know the answers, but we do know the questions, and that we keep on asking them is evidence that human beings are still perplexed by the major issues of truth, reality, God, justice and even happiness.

Perversely perhaps, this lack of practical skills is also what makes philosophers so eminently employable, both in and outside academia. We can read closely and carefully, think critically and constructively, find the forensic flaws in arguments and detect nonsense parading as sense. Do we need more welders than philosophers? Well, that depends what you mean by need.

At which point, we need a philosopher.

15

Brexistentialism

November 6, 2016

LONDON—During these last days of the seemingly endless election campaign, we are all living with enormous and ever-rising levels of anxiety. The days pass in a fever of worry, with waves of nausea that subside only to return and rob us of our breath. Many people are having difficulty sleeping. Many others wake up in fright, their bodies drenched with the sweat of Trump terrors. What will America look like after Tuesday? What will the world look like?

We track the news cycle obsessively, compulsively, trying to find clues that might allow us to know what we cannot know and will not know until Wednesday. We may not know even then. Will Trump accept defeat? What if the election is contested for weeks, months? What if there is civil disorder, with blood in the streets? The waiting is agony.

We constantly press the refresh button on *The Upshot* or whatever lifeline we are clinging to. Foreigners like me try to figure out the possible meaning of those endless sports analogies about field goals. We stare at the screen, look away out of the window and try to focus on something else, and then stare back at the screen again. We pick up handfuls of factoids from the chaos of data that assail us, clutching at the tiny shards of hope glittering on the surface of our media bubble. But we reject them as hopeless, thinking: "He can't really win, can he?" Can he?

The mood of nausea at the world, a disgust at the entirety of existence, is familiar to those of us who cut our teeth reading existentialist fiction. Novels like Sartre's 1938 *Nausea* captured a feeling of disgust with the world and disgust with ourselves for going along with a world so seemingly blissfully happy with itself for so long. For Sartre, the dreadful had already happened, with the rise of National Socialism in the early 1930s: it was a question of learning to face up to our fate. This is the mood that I want to bring into focus by exploring the concept of Brexistentialism.

I must admit, thinking back, that I've become a Brexistentialist of late. That evening of June 23 I watched the entirety—eight hours or more—of the BBC's live coverage of the referendum on whether Britain would leave the European Union or choose to remain.

I was home in New York. As the coverage began, the pollsters, the experts and the markets seemed confident that the good people of Britain would act rationally and vote to remain. And then, with the news of early results from postindustrial northern cities like Sunderland and Newcastle (which are strikingly similar to cities in upstate New York, Ohio, Pennsylvania), one became slowly and dreadfully aware that something else was taking place, something was shifting before one's eyes. By the early hours of the morning of June 24 that smug, smiling, awful face of Nigel Farage was declaring a new dawn, a day of independence for Britain. The supposedly decent, honest, ordinary people of Britain had spoken. The unthinkable had happened.

Will the same thing happen across the Atlantic? No one knows, least of all me. But the parallels are evident, and the anxiety is there, the same nameless dread, that the country that you thought you knew is something and somewhere else entirely. That one's country has unraveled morally and spiritually in such a terribly painful, deeply divisive way.

I arrived in England a few days ago to see family and friends. It's clear that things have changed. The mood has shifted. Everything is dominated by uncertainty. People like my twenty-four-year-old son and his friends feel their future has been stolen from them.

Don't get me wrong. England was hardly ever paradise (on the contrary, which is why I left), but there was a certain self-understanding of the country as being tolerant and open, and a slightly better example of an integrated postcolonial society than any of its neighbors, especially its big brother across the Atlantic. Such beliefs now have been shown to be delusional. Everything here now turns on how one views immigrants and those who don't appear to belong to the core of some regressive idea of Englishness. It seems to me that all this will happen in much more dramatic form in the United States if the unthinkable happens on Tuesday.

The Brexistentialist dread that we are feeling is not an accident. The world is a chaotic, violent place that seems out of joint, confusing and fake. Our blind, simpleminded faith in the power of social media and the allegedly liberating force of the internet has produced a news cycle that cycles ever more bewilderingly out of control. We are endlessly confused by what is going on and disoriented and disgusted by the flood of data that batters us. The distinctions between fact and fiction, truth and falsehood, seem quaint and impossible to parse. Reality has become unreal.

It is this unreal reality that Trump has managed so masterfully—by controlling the news cycle, with the media following along, limply picking up crumbs from his Twitter feed; by constantly changing the message; by pushing the population this way and that with endless revelations; by dissolving the fragile bonds of trust between citizens; by creating a reality where everything is a conspiracy, everything is rigged, where nowhere and no one is safe and we should fear everyone.

Yet, deep in this Brexistential mood, there may be a silver lining. The feeling of dread that we now have in the face of the news cycle and the prospect of a Trump victory is intended to induce powerlessness in those who would oppose Trump. The lesson of existentialism is that the nausea we feel signals the emergence of a genuine, lived sense of freedom. Anxiety is the motor that drives the engine of freedom, and it can take concrete shape in commitment and a vision of collective action in the world. Despite the best and noble efforts of mass movements like Occupy and Black Lives Matter, it is this vision that is missing at the present time and that has to be regained.

Recall Albert Camus's incarnation of Sisyphus, condemned to push a huge rock up a hill for eternity. What interested Camus was the moment when Sisyphus returns to his rock, walking downhill to meet it once again. This was the hour of consciousness for Camus, the moment when Sisyphus is stronger than his rock. The point is not to despair, for that is exactly the reaction that people like Trump want to induce in those who oppose him. The point is to push.

The Tragedy of Violence

16

Euro Blind

November 21, 2011

The past days, weeks and months have seen countless descriptions in the news media of the crisis in the euro zone and Greece's role as its leading actor in the tragedy. But is it a tragedy? Well, yes, but not in the sense in which it is usually discussed, and the difference is important and revealing.

In the usual media parlance, a tragedy is simply a misfortune that befalls a person (an accident, a fatal disease) or a polity (a natural disaster) and that is outside either one's control. While this is an arguably accurate definition of the word—something like it appears in many dictionaries—a deeper and more interesting understanding of the term is to be found in many of the thirty-one extant Greek tragedies.

What these ancient tragedies enact over and over again is not misfortune outside a character's control. Rather, they show the ways in which we humans collude, seemingly unknowingly, with the calamities that befall us.

Tragedy in Greek drama requires some degree of complicity. It is not simply a matter of malevolent fate or a dark prophecy that flows from the inscrutable but often questionable will of the gods. Tragedy requires our collusion with that fate. In other words, it requires a measure of freedom.

It is in this way that we can understand the tragedy of Oedipus. With merciless irony (the first two syllables of the name Oedipus, "the swollen-footed," also mean "I know," *oida*), we watch someone move from a position of seeming knowledge— "I am Oedipus; some call me great; I solve riddles; now, citizens, what seems to be the problem?" (I paraphrase rather freely)—to a deeper truth that it would appear Oedipus knew nothing about: he is a parricide and a perpetrator of incest.

A backstory needs to be recalled. Oedipus turned up in Thebes and solved the Sphinx's riddle only after refusing to return to what he believed was his native Corinth. He refused to return because he had just been given a prophecy about himself by the oracle: that he would kill his father and have sex with his mother.

Oedipus knew his curse. And it is on the way from the oracle that he meets an older man, who actually looks a lot like him—as his mother, Jocasta, inadvertently admits later in the play—who refuses to give way at a crossroads and whom he kills in a fine example of ancient road rage.

One might have thought that, given the awful news from the oracle, and given his uncertainty about the identity of his father (Oedipus is called a bastard by a drunk at a banquet in Corinth, which is what first infects his mind with doubt), he might have exercised caution before deciding to kill an older man. Indeed, a reasonable inference to be drawn from the oracle would have been: "Don't kill older men! You never know who they might be."

One moral aspect of tragedy, then, is that we conspire with our fate. That is, fate requires our freedom in order to bring our destiny down upon us. The tricky paradox of tragedy is that we at one and the same time both know and don't know our fate, and we are destroyed in the process of its reckoning.

Napoleon is alleged to have said to Goethe that the role that fate played in the ancient world was played by the force of politics in the modern world. We no longer require the presence of the gods and oracles to understand the ineluctable power of fate.

This is an interesting thought. But it does not imply that we are condemned to an unswerving fate by the political regimes under which we live. Rather, we conspire with that fate and act—unknowingly, it seems—in such a way as to bring fate down upon our heads. Such is perhaps the life of politics. We get the governments that we deserve.

Keeping the euro crisis in mind, it is notable that tragic drama has a kind of boomerang structure: the action thrown out into the world returns with a potentially fatal velocity. Oedipus, the solver of riddles, becomes the riddle himself. Sophocles's play shows him engaged in a relentless inquiry into the pollution that is destroying the political order, poisoning the wells and producing infant mortality. But he is that pollution.

The deeper truth is that Oedipus knows something of this from the get-go, but he refuses to see and hear what is said to him. Very early in the play, Tiresias, the blind seer, tells him to his face that he is the perpetrator of the pollution that he seeks to eradicate. But Oedipus doesn't hear Tiresias. This is one way of interpreting the word "tyrant" in Sophocles's original Greek title: *Oidipous Tyrannos*. The tyrant doesn't hear what is said to him and doesn't see what is in front of his eyes.

There is a wonderful Greek expression that I borrow here from the poet Anne Carson: "shame lies on the eyelids." The point is that the tyrant experiences no shame. Hosni Mubarak had no shame; Muammar el-Qaddafi had no shame; Silvio Berlusconi has no shame; Rupert Murdoch has no shame.

Greek tragedy provides lessons in shame. For us, learning that lesson and finally achieving some insight, as Oedipus does, must cost us our sight. We might pluck out our eyes—for shame.

The political world is stuffed overfull with sham shame, ham humility and staged tearful apologies. But true shame is something else.

The euro was the very project that was meant to unify Europe and turn a rough amalgam of states in a free market arrangement into a genuine social, cultural and economic unity. But it has ended up disunifying the region and creating perverse effects—such as the spectacular rise of the populist right in countries like the Netherlands—for just about every member state, even dear old Finland.

What makes this a tragedy is that we knew some of the likely consequences all along—economic seers of various stripes had so prophesied—and still, out of arrogance, dogma and complacency, we conspired to push forward. European leaders ignored warnings that the euro was a politically motivated project that would not work given the diversity of economies that the system was meant to cover. The seers, indeed, said it would fail; politicians across Europe ignored the warnings that impugned their version of the fantasy of Europe as a counter-weight to United States' hegemony. Bad deals were made, some lies were told, the peoples of the various member countries were bludgeoned into compliance, often without being consulted, and now the proverbial chickens are coming home to roost.

But we heard nothing and saw nothing, for shame. The tragic truth that we see unspooling in the desperate attempts to shore up the European Union while accepting no responsibility for the unfolding disaster is something that we both willed and that threatens to now destroy the union in its present form.

The euro is a vast boomerang that is busy knocking over millions of people. European leaders, in their blindness, continue to act as if that were not the case.

17

Let Be—An Answer to Hamlet's Question

WITH JAMIESON WEBSTER

July 9, 2011

We could imagine a five-minute version of *Hamlet*.

Scene 1: Hamlet moping at court, dressed in inky black, with a mixture of grief for his dead father and seething loathing for his bloated, boozing uncle, Claudius, who has married his seemingly virtuous mother, Gertrude.

Scene 2: Horatio, a rather close college chum on a surprise visit. The guards turn up and tell Hamlet they've seen his father's perturbed spirit wandering the battlements of Elsinore Castle. Hamlet is amazed and decides to watch for the ghost that night.

Scene 3: The ghost of the father (who of course has the same name as his son) tells Hamlet that he did not die from a serpent bite but was murdered by his brother, Claudius. The ghost asks for vengeance: "Let not the royal bed of Denmark be / a couch for luxury and damned incest."

Scene 4: Hamlet runs from the battlements into the chamber of his "parents" and slaughters Claudius with a rapier and a dagger, but leaves his mother "to heaven"—that is, she gets to live with the prick and sting of bad conscience over what she has done.

Scene 5: Hamlet becomes king of Denmark and defeats the invading armies of Fortinbras. He marries his childhood sweetheart, Ophelia; Laertes is the best man. Gertrude withdraws to a nunnery in England. Polonius meets a younger woman, and the couple hatch the novel idea of founding a Danish colony in the new world: Nova Elsinore.

Exeunt.

What's wrong with this picture? And why, rather than being a five-minute melodrama, is *Hamlet* Shakespeare's longest play? Why, when hearing the truth from the ghost's mouth, is Hamlet able neither to speak of it to anyone unambiguously nor to act on it?

Philosophers, literary critics and psychoanalysts have offered diagnoses for Hamlet's procrastination. For some, Hamlet simply cannot make up his mind: he waits, hesitates and is divided from himself in his "madness," all the while dreaming of a redeeming, cataclysmic violence. In this view, Hamlet is a creature of endless vacillation, a cipher for the alienated inward modern self in a world that is insubstantial and rotten: "Denmark's a prison," Hamlet sighs. For others, Hamlet is the great melancholic who is jealous of Claudius for realizing his own secret desire—to usurp the place of his rival in the affection of his mother.

For still others, Hamlet is not so much a bather in the black sun of depression but rather too much a bather in the sun of knowledge. Through the medium of the ghost, he has grasped his nature and that of his family and the corrupt political order that surrounds him. Here, Hamlet is a kind of anti-Oedipus: whereas the latter moves ragefully from ignorance to knowledge (and his insight requires the loss of his sight in an act of self-blinding), the great Dane knows the score from the beginning.

But his knowledge does not lead to action. Perhaps action requires veils of illusion, and once those veils are lifted, resignation sets in.

Whatever the truth of these various interpretations—and much can to be said for each of them—there seems to be a significant disconnection between thought and action in the person of Hamlet. Consider the famous "To be, or not to be" soliloquy. After contemplating suicide as an attempted "quietus" from a "weary life," Hamlet ponders the dread of life after death, "the undiscovered country," and how pondering the afterlife saps the will and makes us endure our present sufferings rather than risk ones we do not know. He continues:

> Thus conscience does make cowards of us all,
> And thus the native hue of resolution
> Is sicklied over with the pale cast of thought,
> And enterprises of great pitch and moment,
> With this regard their currents turn awry
> And lose the name of action.

Thought and action seem to pull against each other, the former annulling the possibility of the latter. If, as Hamlet says elsewhere, "there is nothing either good or bad but thinking makes it so," then thinking seems to make things rather bad for him. Resolution dissolves into thin air. Speaking of thin air, we might notice that when the ghost makes his second and final appearance, in a scene of almost unbearable verbal and near-physical violence, with Hamlet raging at his mother for her inconstancy, he says, "This visitation / is but to whet thy almost blunted purpose." Hamlet confesses to being a "tardy son" who has not committed "Th' important acting" of the ghost's command.

The ghost, stepping between Hamlet and his mother, asks Hamlet to step between her and her fighting soul and speak.

For a moment it seems as if he might say, "Dear mother, you are sleeping with your husband's murderer." But as she mumbles the word "ecstasy," Hamlet careens into the most pathetic of adjurations, begging Gertrude not to sleep again with Claudius, but then he gives up and accuses her of conceit. "Conceit in weakest bodies strongest works," the ghost says.

The only apparent way Hamlet can attempt to close the gap between thought and action is through the ultimate conceit—that is, through theater itself, through play. The purpose of *The Mousetrap*, the play within the play in act 3, is to produce a thing that will catch the conscience of the king. But, as Hamlet is acutely aware—and as, one naively presumes, that enigma we call Shakespeare lurking in the wings is even more acutely aware—a play is nothing, at least nothing real. It is, rather, "a fiction . . . a dream of passion." Theater is "all for nothing." What are the sufferings of Hecuba, or indeed Hamlet, to us? Yet Hamlet would seem to be suggesting that the fictional ground of theater is the only vehicle in which the truth might be presented. As A. C. Bradley said, Hamlet is the only Shakespearean character who we could think had written Shakespeare's plays.

The trap works and the mouse-king's conscience is caught. The dumb show reenactment of Hamlet Senior's murder pricks the king's conscience, and he flees the theater calling for "light." We then find Claudius alone confessing his fratricidal crime: "O, my offense is rank." On the way to his mother's bedroom, to which he's been summoned, Hamlet passes Claudius kneeling in futile prayer. With Claudius genuflecting, head bowed, Hamlet could, with one swoop of his sword, reconcile thought and action and avenge his father. But at that precise moment, Hamlet begins to think and decides that this is the wrong moment to kill Claudius because he is at prayer and trying to make his amends with heaven. It is "hire and salary," he says, "not revenge." Hamlet fantasizes about killing Claudius at the right moment, "When he is drunk asleep, or in his rage, or in th' incestuous pleasure of his bed." He sheathes his sword and moves quickly to meet his mother.

It is not that Hamlet cannot act. He kills Polonius, Rosencrantz and Guildenstern, Ophelia (in a certain fashion), and eventually Claudius, too. But the first death is inadvertent—he hears a noise from behind the arras, strikes and then insouciantly asks, "Is it the king?" having just left Claudius alive seconds earlier. Rosencrantz and Guildenstern die in his stead offstage, an act of self-preservation that even impressed Freud given Hamlet's otherwise massive inhibition. Poor Ophelia's suicide is something like a tragic casualty of Hamlet's unrelenting cruelty toward her—his killing of her father is the coup de grâce in her unfolding psychosis. And the intended victim, Claudius, is murdered only when Hamlet has been hit with the poisoned rapier and knows that he himself is going to die: "I am dead, Horatio," he repeats in three variations in a little over twenty lines. The dying Laertes spills the beans about the plot with the poisoned rapiers and wine—"the king's to blame"—and Hamlet stabs Claudius to death after just one line's reflection, "The point envenomed too? / Then venom, to thy work!"

If thought kills action, then action must be thoughtless— such would appear to be Hamlet's credo. The cost of Hamlet's infinite self-reflexivity is incapacity of action. Such is the curse of self-consciousness, which gives us extraordinary insight into ourselves, but its companions are melancholy, alienation and paralysis. Another consequence: there is little left to Hamlet of eros. So follows the savage dissolution of Ophelia as his object of love.

Is that it? Are we left with the unanswerable ontological question "To be, or not to be?" Or, "if philosophy could find it out," might there not be another moral to draw from the play? A different line of thought is suggested by the deeply

enigmatic speech given to the ever-trusty Horatio just before
Hamlet fights with Laertes in a conflict that he intuits will cost
him his life.

> We defy augury. There's a special providence in the
> fall of a sparrow. If it be now, 'tis not to come. If it
> be not to come, it will be now. If it be not now, yet
> it will come. The readiness is all. Since no man, of
> aught he leaves, knows aught, what is't to leave
> betimes? Let be.

Generations of readers have interpreted these lines in
relation to a Christian idea of Providence and linked them to
Hamlet's earlier words, "There is a divinity that shapes our ends."
This might be correct, but perhaps these words can withstand
another, slightly more skeptical gloss.

My thought here is that a possible response to the question
"To be, or not to be?" is "Let be." What might that mean? The
defiance of augury, or omen, is most interesting in the preceding passage, the refusal of any ability on our part to predict the
future, to foresee the course of events. But if we cannot predict
the future, the second verse might be intended slightly ironi-
cally: "What, you mean, there's a special providence in the fall
of a sparrow?" The point might be that if there is any providence
at work, we know nothing of it. Such knowledge is the unique
attribute of the divinity of whom we mere mortals can know
nothing, rough-hew him or her how we will. Knowing nothing,
letting be, means for Hamlet that "the readiness is all." Is this,
then, how we might understand the knot of negations that crowd
the next lines of the text? If it be now, then it is not to come,
and if it is to come, then it is not now. The wisdom here seems
close to what Epicurus says: When death is, I am not; when I
am, death is not; therefore, why worry?

Perhaps the gap between thought and action can never be bridged. And perhaps this is the lesson of Hamlet for modern philosophy and for us. But such skepticism is not a reason for either depression or the "antic disposition" of seeming madness, Hamlet's endless oscillation between melancholia and mania. It might allow for something else—for example, the rather grim humor that punctuates *Hamlet*. Think of the Dane's endless puns and the extraordinary scene between Hamlet and the clown who also doubles as a gravedigger. Everyone knows the "Alas, poor Yorick" speech, but what is less well known is the way Alexander the Great becomes the bunghole in a beer barrel. Hamlet provides the precise reasoning:

> Alexander died, Alexander was buried, Alexander returneth into dust, the dust is earth, of earth we make loam and why of that loam, whereto he was converted, might they not stop a beer-barrel?

If we are Hamlet-like creatures, divided against ourselves between thought and action, perhaps this division can be borne by humor, indeed, by a rather noir comic realism.

The readiness is all, provided we can cultivate a disposition of skeptical openness that does not claim to know aught of what we truly know naught. If we can cure ourselves of our longing for some sort of godlike conspectus of what it means to be human, or our longing for the construction of ourselves as some new prosthetic god through technology, bound by the self-satisfied myth of unlimited human progress, we might let be. This, I would insist, is why we need theater, especially tragedy, to "absent thee from felicity awhile."

In Hamlet's final words, "The rest is silence."

18

The Cycle of Revenge

September 8, 2011

I've never understood the proverbial wisdom that revenge is a dish best served cold. Some seem to like it hot. Better is the Chinese proverb, attributed to Confucius, "Before you embark on a journey of revenge, dig two graves." Osama bin Laden's grave was watery (he was buried at sea), but the other still appears empty. Is it intended for us?

Revenge is the desire to repay an injury or a wrong by inflicting harm, often the violent sort. If you hit me, I will hit you back. Furthermore, by the logic of revenge, I am right to hit you back. The initial wrong justifies the act of revenge. But does that wrong really make it right for me to hit back? Once we act out of revenge, don't we become mired in a cycle of violence and counterviolence with no apparent end? Such is arguably our current predicament.

Moving from ends to beginnings brings us to the other peculiarity of revenge: that it is often unclear who committed the first wrong or threw the first stone. If someone, George W. Bush, say, asserts that the United States is justified in revenging itself on Al Qaeda by invading Afghanistan, then Iraq, and in carrying on the rest of the brutal saga of the past ten years, what would Bin Laden have said? Well, the opposite, of course.

In a scarily fascinating 2004 video called *The Towers of Lebanon,* in which Bin Laden claims direct responsibility for 9/11 for the first time, he says that the September 11 attacks were justified as an act of revenge. Since the United States violated the security of the Muslim world—especially by using his homeland of Saudi Arabia as a base during the first Gulf War— then Al Qaeda was justified in violating American security. If there had been no initial violation, he claims, there would have been no need for revenge. Bin Laden contrasts the United States with Sweden: Because the Swedes have never been aggressors in the Muslim world, he says, they have nothing to fear from Al Qaeda.

Bin Laden then reveals the extraordinary fact that the idea for 9/11 originated in his visual memory of the 1982 Israeli bombardments of West Beirut's high-rise apartment blocks. He recalls his intense reaction to seeing images of the destroyed towers and formed the following notion: "It occurred to me to punish the oppressor in kind by destroying towers in America." ("Missile into towers," he might have whispered; the idea stuck.) The September 11 attacks, which most of us remember as a series of visual images, repeatedly televised and published, originated from an earlier series of images. For Bin Laden, there was a strange kind of visual justice in 9/11, the retributive paying back of an image for an image, an eye for an eye.

Opposites attract—the awful violence of 9/11 is justified by Al Qaeda as an act of revenge that in turn justifies the violence of America's and Bush's revenge. My point is that revenge is an inevitably destructive motive for action. When we act out of revenge, revenge is what we will receive in return. The wheel of violence and counterviolence spins without end and leads inevitably to destruction.

This is exactly what Bin Laden hoped to bring about. He admits that Al Qaeda spent $500,000 on the 9/11 attacks and estimates that the United States lost, at the lowest estimate, $500 billion in the event and the aftermath. He even does the math: "That makes a million American dollars for every Al Qaeda dollar, by the grace of God Almighty." He concludes, ominously, "This shows the success of our plan to bleed America to the point of bankruptcy, with God's will."

Like it or not (I don't like it at all), Bin Laden had a point. The last ten years of unending war on terror has also led, at least partly, to the utter financial precariousness that we see at every level of life in the United States, federal, state, city and individual, all laden with debt. We are bankrupt.

But why grant Bin Laden some sick posthumous victory? Consider an alternative scenario.

In a 1999 Republican debate George W. Bush, then a candidate, responded—to the accompaniment of complacent guffaws from liberals—to a question about which political philosopher he most identified with. "Christ, because he changed my heart," Bush said. In that case, it was fair to wonder what Jesus might have recommended in response to 9/11. The answer is clear: Turn the other cheek.

In the New Testament, Peter asks Jesus about the quantity of forgiveness: How many times should he forgive someone who had sinned against him? Is seven times enough? To which Jesus replies, from his full messianic height, "No, not seven times, but seventy times seven," meaning that there is no quantity to forgiveness, just an infinite quality.

Think back ten years, if you will. In the days and weeks that followed 9/11 the people of New York City, Washington, DC, and indeed the entire United States were the recipients of an unquantifiable wave of empathy from across the world. The initial effect of 9/11 (I was still living in England at the time) was the confirmation in the minds of many millions of people that New York was an extraordinary place that rightly engendered huge affection, indeed love.

Ask yourself: What if nothing had happened after 9/11? No revenge, no retribution, no failed surgical strikes on the Afghanistan-Pakistan border, no poorly planned bloody fiasco in Iraq, no surges and no insurgencies to surge against; nothing.

What if the government had decided to turn the other cheek and forgive those who sought to attack it, not seven times, but seventy times seven? What if the grief and mourning that followed 9/11 were allowed to foster a nonviolent ethics of compassion rather than a violent politics of revenge and retribution? What if the crime of the September 11 attacks had led not to an unending war on terror but to the cultivation of a practice of peace—a difficult, fraught and ever-compromised endeavor, but perhaps worth the attempt?

As we know all too well, this didn't happen. Instead, all of that glorious global fellow feeling was wasted and allowed to dissipate in acts of revenge that have bankrupted this country, both financially and spiritually.

Perhaps the second grave is ours. We dug it ourselves. The question now is: Do we have to lie in it?

19

Theater of Violence

WITH BRAD EVANS

March 14, 2016

BRAD EVANS: I want to start the discussion by raising a seemingly basic yet elusive question: What actually *is* violence? In terms of media spectacles and popular culture, violence seems ubiquitous in liberal societies. Yet the very term "violence" continually escapes meaningful definition and critique. What do you understand by the term?

SIMON CRITCHLEY: It is true, "violence" can be used in a very wide and somewhat vague manner. So let me try and restrict our discussion to physical violence of a rather direct form. Let's say that violence is behavior that uses physical force to cause damage, harm or death to some living thing, whether human or not. It is pretty clear that we are not all going to be able to agree on a definition of violence, but let's see where this idea of it takes us.

Violence cannot be reduced to an isolated act that could be justified with reference to some conception or principle of justice. Here I borrow a line of thought from the historian and cultural theorist Robert Young when he writes that violence "is a phenomenon that has a history." Violence is not so much a question of a single act that breaks a supposed continuum of nonviolence or peace. Rather, violence is best understood as a historical cycle of violence and counterviolence. In other words, violence is not one but two. It is a double act that traps human beings in a repetitive pattern from which it is very hard to escape. Violence, especially political violence, is usually a pattern of aggression and counteraggression that has a history and that stretches back deep into time.

This is how I would understand the patterns involving race and racialized violence that have taken on added urgency of late. Violence is not an abstract concept for those subjected to it but a lived reality which has a concrete history. To try and judge the racial violence that defines current life in the United States without an understanding of the history of violence that stretches back to colonization, the forced transport of Africans to the colonies of the Americas and the implementation of plantation slavery is largely pointless. We have to understand the history of violence from which we emerge.

B.E.: In that respect, as your colleague Richard Bernstein has argued, even massive historical events like the September 11 attacks don't necessarily provoke serious thinking on the problem of violence.

s.c.: One way of looking at 9/11—let's call it the standard way—is that the United States was at peace with the world and then terror came from the sky and the twin towers tumbled. On that view, 9/11 was a single act that required a justified reaction: war in the Middle East, the infinite detention of suspected "terrorists" in places like Guantánamo Bay and the construction of the vast institutional apparatus of Homeland Security.

But another way of looking at 9/11 is to see what Osama bin Laden said about the matter. As I write in "The Cycle of Revenge," Bin Laden justifies the attacks by claiming that they were a reaction to the persistent violation of Arab lands by the United States, especially the use of Saudi Arabia as a base during the first Gulf War. The idea of 9/11 came to him as a visual memory after watching TV footage of the Israeli bombardment of West Beirut's high-rise apartment blocks in 1982. If the "Zionist-Crusaders," as he pejoratively puts it, could put missiles into towers, then so could Al Qaeda. Thus the idea for 9/11 was born.

The point is that if we are to understand violence concretely, then we have to grasp it historically as part of a cycle of action and reaction, violence and counterviolence, that always stretches back further than one thinks. If one doesn't do this, one ends up like Donald Trump, emptily promising to flatten ISIS with bombs. It's in this light that we might also consider the theater of Trump that has exploded with truly disturbing and racially coded violence in recent times.

B.E.: If violence shouldn't be theorized in the abstract, as you rightly insist, we must pay attention to how it is enacted. In this, the importance of theater, which is a recurring theme throughout your work, is often overlooked. What do you think theater has to offer here?

S.C.: We live in a world framed by violence, where justice seems to be endlessly divided between claim and counterclaim, right and left, freedom fighter and terrorist, believer and nonbeliever, and so on. Each side appears to believe unswervingly in the rightness of its position and the wrongness, or indeed "evil," of the opposition. Such belief legitimates violence and unleashes counterviolence in return. We seem to be trapped in deep historical cycles of violence where justice is usually understood as vengeance or revenge.

This is where theater can help, especially tragedy (but I think this is also true of the best movies and TV dramas).

It is useful to consider the Greeks. The history of Greek tragedy is the history of violence and war, from the war with

the Persians in the early fifth century BCE to the Peloponnesian
War that runs until that century's end, from the emergence of
Athenian imperial hegemony to its dissolution and humiliation
at the hands of Sparta. In 472 BCE, in the oldest extant play we
possess, *The Persians,* Aeschylus deals with the aftermath of the
Battle of Salamis in 480. It was therefore somewhat closer to
the Athenians than 9/11 is to us. More than half of our surviving Greek tragedies were composed after the outbreak of the
Peloponnesian War in 431. *Oedipus the King* was first performed
in 429, two years after the beginning of the war, during a time
of plague. The plague that established the entire environment
of Sophocles's play is not some idle musing. It was very real
indeed. It is estimated to have killed one-quarter of the Athenian
population. It killed Pericles, the leader of Athens, that very
same year. The frame of tragedy is war and its devastating effects
on human life.

Greek tragedy, particularly with its obsessive focus on
the aftermath of the Trojan War, is largely *about* combat veterans. But it was also performed *by* combat veterans. Actors were
not flimsy thespians or the Athenian version of Hollywood
stars but soldiers who had seen combat, like Aeschylus himself.
They knew firsthand what violence was. Tragedy was played
before an audience that either had participated directly in war
or were indirectly implicated in war. All were traumatized by
it, and everyone felt its effects. War was the life of the city and
its pride, as Pericles argued. But war was also the city's fall and
undoing.

How might we respond in a similar way to the contemporary situation of violence and war? It might seem that the
easiest and noblest thing to do is to speak of peace. Yet, as
Raymond Williams says in his still hugely relevant 1966 book,
Modern Tragedy, "to say peace when there is no peace is to
say nothing." The danger of easy pacifism is that it is inert and

self-regarding. It is always too pleased with itself. But the alternative is not a justification of war. It is rather the attempt to understand the deep history and tragic complexity of political situations.

The great virtue of ancient tragedy is that it allowed the Greeks to see their role in a history of violence and war that was to some extent of their own making. It also allowed them to imagine a suspension of that cycle of violence. And this suspension, the kind of thing that happens in the trial at the end of Aeschylus's *Oresteia*, was not based on a fanciful idealism but on a realistic and concrete grasp of a historical situation, which was something the Greeks did by focusing history through the lens of myth.

The slim slither of hope I have is that the same could be true of us. To see the bloody events of the contemporary world in a tragic light exposes us to a disorder that is not just someone else's disorder. It is *our* disorder, and theater at its best asks us to take the time to reflect on this and to imagine what a world where violence is suspended might look like.

B.E.: With that in mind, I'd like now to turn to Shakespeare. In *Stay, Illusion! The Hamlet Doctrine* you show how Shakespearean figures are relevant for understanding the ways in which deeply tragic questions concerning life, death and love are embodied today. What is it about Shakespeare that still captures the violence of the times?

S.C.: From the beginning to the end, Shakespeare's drama is a meditation on political violence. Whether one thinks of the wild excesses of *Titus Andronicus,* the vast majestic sweep of the history plays, or the great tragedies, Shakespeare had a tight and commanding grip on the nature of political power and its relation to violence and the claims and counterclaims of justice. What is most powerful about Shakespeare is the way his historically coded reflections on the politics of his time are combined with intense and immense psychological intimacy. Shakespeare, like no one before or since, binds together the political and the psychological.

It is not just that the play I know best, *Hamlet,* is a drama of violence in a surveillance state where power is constituted through acts of murder (the Castle of Elsinore and the state of Denmark are clearly allegories of some sort for the late Elizabethan court and a police state). It is also that we feel an awful proximity to the effects of violence on the mind of the young Danish prince and the way it drives his feigned madness into something more real and frightening, as when he confronts his mother with terrifying psychical violence (act 3, scene 4).

What answer does *Hamlet* give that helps us understand our current political situation? Simply put, the play counsels us that time is out of joint. What people often forget is that Hamlet's father, before he was himself murdered, killed Fortinbras's father. And therefore it is fitting that *Hamlet* ends not just with the prince's death but with the military occupation of Denmark by the forces of young Fortinbras, who is Hamlet's twin insofar as they are both the sons of murdered fathers, one by the other.

So the point of Shakespeare is not to give us simple answers or reassuring humanistic moral responses to violence, but to get us to confront the violence of our own histories. *Hamlet* gives us many warnings, but perhaps the most salient is the following: If we imagine that justice is based on vengeance against others, then we are truly undone.

B.E.: How can we connect insights such as this to the historical and evidently prescient contemporary relationship between violence and sport? Are sporting arenas perhaps the real theaters of our times? Are they inevitably bound up with the problem of violence in both its glorified and its vilified forms?

S.C.: Ah, now you're talking. Sport is obviously the continuation of war by other means. And sports stadiums are undoubtedly the closest thing to ancient theaters that we have, especially in terms of scale (nearly fifteen thousand people sat in the Theater of Dionysos in Athens). It's fascinating to me that when Bertolt Brecht was trying to imagine the ideal audience for the kind of epic theater he was developing in the 1920s, he pictured a sports crowd. That is, a crowd that is relaxed and not anxious, that is sitting under lights rather than in the dark and that has knowledge of what is happening and a passion for it. People in New York theaters usually either look perplexed or quietly take naps. I think there is a lot to Brecht's idea.

Sport is obviously violent, and it is violence that we want to see. We want to see people putting their bodies on the line for their team and leaving their bodies on the field. This is why the whole debate about concussions in the NFL is so hypo-critical, to my mind. Sport is a place where bodies break. If you don't agree with it, don't watch it.

But a game is not just some gladiatorial spectacle of violence. Sport is violence honed into skill and masterful expertise, what psychoanalysts would call sublimation. It is violence re-fined and elevated. And sporting drama is made possible only through an elaborate set of rules, which have to be observed and with which all parties agree.

But what is in the background of the rule-governed physical violence of sport is something more complex, some-thing closer to what the ancients called fate. This is particu-larly the case with the sport that you and I hold dearest, what our American pals call soccer. For the real fan, what is at stake in a soccer match is a sense of profound attachment to place, whether town, city or nation, a sense of identity that is almost tribal and that is often organized around social class, ethnicity, dialect or language. But what is driving the whole activity is something closer to destiny. This sense is usually experienced when one's team loses, when one has the sinking feeling that

England must lose when playing Germany and the game has to end with penalty shots.

But the key phenomenon of sport in relation to violence is that although sport can and does spill over into actual violence (whether through hooliganism or ethnic or racist violence), this usually doesn't happen. As a fan, one follows the physical, violent intensity of the game with a mixture of intense passion and expert knowledge of what is happening, and then the game ends and one goes home, often a little disappointed. I think sport, especially soccer, is a wonderful example of how violence can be both made spectacular and harnessed for nonviolent ends. Ideally, one accepts defeat, respects the opponent and moves on eagerly to the next game.

B.E.: The subtlety of the potential for nonviolence you express here seems crucial. In particular, how might we develop the necessary intellectual tools adequate to these deeply violent and politically fraught times?

S.C.: My response is very simple: art. I think that art at its most resonant and powerful can give us an account of the history of violence from which we emerge and can also offer us the possibility of a suspension of that violence. Art can provide an image for our age.

For me, this happens most powerfully in popular music. For me, as for many others, one of the most coherent and powerful responses to the racialized violence of the past year or so was Kendrick Lamar's *To Pimp a Butterfly*. With dazzling linguistic inventiveness, steeped in an intense inward knowledge of the traditions of jazz, soul and funk, Lamar does not provide easy solutions or empty moral platitudes but confronts us aesthetically with the deep history of racialized violence. You hear this very clearly on a track like "Alright." It is what Public Enemy, Curtis Mayfield and Marvin Gaye did so powerfully in previous generations.

Some days I am inclined to agree with Nietzsche when he said that without music life would be error. Music like Lamar's doesn't give us the answers, but it allows us to ask the right questions, and it does this with a historical and political sensibility suffused with intelligence, wit and verve. Great music can give us a picture of the violence of our time more powerfully than any news report. It can also offer, for the time that we listen, a momentary respite from the seemingly unending cycles of violence and let us imagine some other way of being, something less violent, less vengeful and less stupid.

Athens in Pieces

20

The Art of Memory

January 30, 2019

ATHENS—The art of memory, legend says, began with the poet Simonides of Ceos (556–468 BCE). Simonides was giving a recitation in the dining hall of the house of Scopas, a Thessalian nobleman, when he was called outside because two strangers wanted to speak to him.

When the poet exited, the strangers were nowhere to be found, and the dining hall suddenly and violently collapsed. Scopas and his guests were crushed to death and disfigured beyond recognition. But Simonides was able to identify each of the corpses by remembering the precise place where they were sitting or lounging before the calamity.

With this association of memory with place, or topos, the idea of mnemotechnics, or the art of memory, came into being. To recall something, one has to either identify a locus in the interior palace of one's memory or construct an exterior, physical memory theater. Various attempts to build such memory theaters punctuate antiquity. The practice was picked up again in the Italian Renaissance, is evident in the architecture of Elizabethan theater—like Shakespeare's Globe—and continues today.

The story of Simonides is somewhat grisly, but I would like to borrow the association of recollection and location to build a tiny—and admittedly idiosyncratic—memory theater of Athens, a personal cabinet of memory spaces and places: treasures, oddities and curiosities. Every city, every polis, is a necropolis, a city of the dead; but it just so happens that Athens is a particularly ancient graveyard with multiple, interconnected and entangled layers of life that has passed away. Its ghosts continue to haunt our present, often in unexpected and unimagined ways. And for those of us who have spent time trying to teach philosophy, Athens is a magical city, for this is where what we still recognize as philosophia really began.

How do we make those ancient Athenian ghosts speak to us? How is it possible to revive what is dead? In a lecture given in Oxford in 1908, the famous German philologist Ulrich von Wilamowitz-Moellendorff said, "We know that ghosts cannot speak until they have drunk blood; and the spirits which we evoke demand the blood of our hearts. We give it to them gladly." To revive the ancients, we have to give them a little of our lifeblood (although I hope reading these essays won't be too bloody painful).

The consequence of Wilamowitz-Moellendorff's thought is that the blood that flows in the veins of these ancient ghosts is our own and that, therefore, when the ancients speak to us, they tell us not just about themselves but also about us. We always see antiquity in the image of ourselves and our age. But that image is not some Narcissus-like reflection; it is more of an oblique refraction that allows us to see ourselves in a novel way and in a slightly alien manner. By looking into the deep past, we see ourselves, but perhaps not as we have seen ourselves before, turned inside out and upside down.

This touches on the reason I decided to attempt a newspaper column on philosophy. The world, especially that corner of it that we still call the West, has become a deafening place dominated by an ever-enlarging incoherence of information and the constant presence of verbal and physical violence. Our countries are split, our houses are divided and the fragile web of family and friendship withers under the black sun of big tech. Everything that passed as learning seems to have reached a boiling point. We simmer, we feel the heat and we wonder what can be done.

Now, something I have noticed here and there when talking to sundry folk over the past couple of years is a renewed interest in antiquity: Greek, Roman, Babylonian, Chinese, Mayan, or whatever. This is partly because the ancient past offers some kind of solace and escape from the seeming urgency of the present—and such consolation cannot be disregarded. Antiquity can be the source of immense pleasure: the word feels almost scandalous to employ. For a time, we can be transported elsewhere, where life was formed by different forces and shaped with patterns slightly alien to our own.

But also—and most importantly—the ancient past can give us a way of pushing back against what Wallace Stevens called the "pressure of reality," of enlivening the leadenness of the present with the transforming force of the historical imagination. Antiquity, then, can provide us with breathing space, perhaps even an oxygen tank, where we can fill our lungs before plunging back into the blips, tweets, clicks, and endless breaking news updates that populate our days, a locus where we are "distracted from distraction by distraction," as T. S. Eliot said. By looking into the past, we can see further and more clearly into the present.

Having emphasized the connection between memory and location, let me tell you something about the place where I am writing these essays, as it is rather grand.

I have a desk and a lamp (and access to strong Greek coffee) in the Onassis Foundation Library, close to Hadrian's Arch.

Out of the window, across the near constant hum of thick traffic on Syngrou Avenue, I can see the vast columns of the Temple of Olympian Zeus. Their tall Corinthian capitals shine in the cool winter sun. The library is a mere slingshot distance from the Acropolis and a truly privileged spot in which to work. I am sitting across from the first printed edition of Homer's *Opera*, which was published by Greek printers in Florence in 1488–89, and the *Etymologicum Magnum*, which was the first printed lexical encyclopedia in Greek, produced by Cretan printers in Venice in 1499. There are many other dizzyingly beautiful treasures in this library, which was based on the personal collection of Konstantinos Sp. Staikos.

I met with Mr. Staikos in the library last week. He is also an architect, and he designed the library in which we sat. He is a person of great erudition and carefully chosen words, and I could not help but be impressed. We talked for a long while about the history of libraries in the Hellenic world and their connection to the various philosophical schools of Athens and elsewhere. My mind began to whir and spin with possibility. For a library is also a memory theater. Being inside this library is a little like being inside the head of Mr. Staikos, and I have spent the last week reading his many volumes on the history of libraries, where he offers detailed architectural reconstructions of their design, their function and even their holdings.

One of Mr. Staikos's lifelong passions is the attempt to reconstruct the library and the entire architecture of Plato's Academy from the fourth century BCE. This is the topic of next week's essay, "The Stench of the Academy."

As for the other objects to be discussed, I would like them to be a bit of a surprise. This is mostly because I am intent on letting Athens surprise me. I am not at all sure what the coming weeks will hold in their storehouse of memory.

21

The Stench of the Academy

February 5, 2019

The weekend traffic in the center of Athens was awful on the late January day I decided to visit the site of Plato's Academy. Each of the narrow, slightly doglegged streets in Plaka, the old city, was completely jammed because recent angry protests, some of them violent, had forced the closing of roads around Syntagma, or Constitution Square.

Still, pedestrians were out in impressive force, filling the streets, intent on enjoying their Saturday shopping. Athenians take their weekends seriously. Pantelis, my cabdriver, threaded his way delicately around people lurching, semi-oblivious, into the street and the motorcycles appearing out of nowhere and disappearing noisily into the distance.

Once past the clogged junction at Monastiraki Square, we pushed more easily along Ermou Street and headed northwest. We came to an area scattered with warehouses and former factories. The cab stopped by a huddle of abandoned buses. Ahead of us was what looked like an open area of greenery. Pantelis pointed and said, "Akadimia Platonos." This must be the place, I thought.

Plato's Academy is now a public park in a not particularly nice part of town. It is just next to Colonus, Sophocles's birthplace and, according to the legend Plato helped to invent, the final resting place of Oedipus. The day was cool and sunny, but the previous forty-eight hours had been filled with storms, strong winds and intense rain.

Where I entered the park from the south, the ground was muddy with large puddles. My boots slipped and slid as I made my way past a man talking loudly on a cell phone in what I think was Bengali. A couple were playing in the distance with their dog. There was an empty playground and a rather nice gravel area for playing pétanque, which is apparently popular with the locals. It was deserted.

I oriented myself with notes and guidebooks and made my way to the ruins of the Gymnasium, which is thought to have been the main building of the Academy. A large grassy hollow indicated the site of a former archaeological dig. I peered through some trees into the open green area of the ruins. A solitary man stood there, reflectively smoking a huge joint; what appeared to be a bottle of water was at his feet. In fact, the only people I saw around the various ruins were doing exactly the same thing as this man: quietly getting wasted at a Saturday lunchtime. I began to doubt whether the liquid was water, for these men didn't have the appearance of compulsive Brooklyn yoga hydrators. Ah, the sacred groves of academe!

After a moment's hesitation, I walked down into the ruins, exchanged a brief *"ya sass"* (hello) with the man, who didn't seem to care in the slightest that I was there. It was very quiet, and all around was a calming, low chatter of birds. No riots here.

I began to try to imagine the Academy.

The school, founded by Plato around 387 BCE, was named the Hecademia and later the Academia after the nearby sanctuary dedicated to the hero Hecademus. In Plato's time, the area occupied about three and a half acres and was reached by leaving the city of Athens by the Diplon gate and walking along a road flanked by a public cemetery. The Gymnasium was a rectangular complex, approximately two hundred feet long and one hundred feet wide. For me, standing in the ruins, the scale of the building felt larger than I had anticipated. The site was excavated in 1929–39 and a plan of the main building was published.

An open courtyard, or atrium, was surrounded on three sides by a roofed single-story colonnade, or peristyle, which may have provided shelter for academicians engaged in reading and copying papyri or perhaps just passing the time. In the middle of the atrium stood a cistern, which supplied water, and farther north are the remains of a pedestal on which stood statues of the nine Muses, the goddesses of the arts and letters.

The Academy is now both a museum and a temple or sacred space; the association is continued in Aristotle's Lyceum and in the most famous library of the ancient world: the Museum of Alexandria, founded by the Ptolemies after 297 BCE (the building once contained the famous and famously destroyed library).

Behind the Muses was the main building of the Academy, divided into a number of rooms. We are not exactly sure of their function, but it is highly likely that they were used for teaching and were equipped with boards, writing materials, geometric instruments, globes and celestial spheres. But the center of the Academy was the library, well stocked with texts, stacked papyri, possibly with labels on which the titles were inscribed. The library was the first of its kind in Athens.

To delve a little deeper, here's an intriguing question: What was on the shelves of Plato's library? What had he read, and what did he give his students to read? We can only guess, but it's likely there would have been writings on mathematics,

geometry and medicine, volumes by Homer and Hesiod. From
the dialogues, it is clear that Plato had read the now long-lost
works of pre-Socratic thinkers like Heraclitus (*On Nature*) and
Anaxagoras (*Nous*) and texts by Eleatic thinkers like Par-
menides. It is also said that Plato made an extremely expensive
purchase of three works by Pythagoras. There would also have
been works by the Sophists, whom Plato loathed, and possibly
the widely read works of the atomists, like Democritus, whom
Plato completely ignored, possibly out of envy.

In addition to the bookshelves storing these texts, there
was possibly a wooden dais for the readings, lectures and discussions that took place daily. Most intriguing perhaps in the
design of the Academy is the House of the Reader. It is said that
a young Aristotle served as the anagnostes—reader or lector—
during his twenty years in the Academy. Apparently, he was
nicknamed Nous (Mind) by Plato, which seems appropriate.
The anagnostic reader was apparently responsible for reading
aloud every treatise submitted for publication in the Academy.

The striking wholly geometric design of the Academy, my
new friend, Mr. Staikos, thinks, was due to the influence of the
Pythagorean school, which Plato encountered on his trips to
Sicily and which had been revived by Archytas of Taras, a friend
of Plato's who was, some say, the model for the philosopher-king
described in the *Republic*. Legend has it that the motto of the
Academy, written over the entrance, was "Let no one ignorant
of geometry enter." For the Academy is not just a building. It
is also an idea in accordance with Plato's theory of the forms
and the Pythagorean view that ultimate reality is expressed by
numbers.

The Academy was also a privately funded research and
teaching facility, situated outside the city. Most of us have a
rather whimsical idea of philosophy as a bunch of men in togas
having a chat in the agora. And we think of Socrates as a gadfly,

philosophizing in the street and somehow speaking truth to power. The idea is attractive. But it is a literary conceit of philosophy—one that is still in circulation today. It is the fiction that Plato wanted his readers to believe.

Behind that fiction stands the library, the editing and copying rooms, and the entire research engine of the Academy, which was devoted to the careful production and dissemination of knowledge through texts and teaching. Much as we may flinch at the idea, philosophy has been academic and linked to the activity of schools since its inception.

At this point, a rather vulgar question comes to mind: Who paid for the Academy? According to Mr. Staikos, the cost of construction is estimated at twenty-five to thirty talents. As a wild modern-day estimate, we could say that the Academy cost a couple of hundred thousand dollars to build. How did Plato get this money? We don't know. It is said that he was captured on his return trip from Sicily in 387 and sold as a slave on the island of Aegina, which Athens was at war with at the time. According to one account, Anniceris of Cyrene paid a ransom of thirty minas. But he refused to be paid back after Plato was returned to Athens, and the money was used to pay for the plot of land where the Academy was built.

Although the splendidly unreliable Diogenes Laertius says that Plato possessed no property other than that mentioned in his will, Plato received a large sum of money from Dionysius I. Indeed, Plato had a significant fund of money at his disposal (the exorbitant figure of eighty talents is mentioned). Plato is also said to have had at his service a banker called Andromedes. In other words, Plato was rich and had wealthy patrons and very probably wealthy students.

We are less attracted to the idea of a wealthy aristocratic philosopher sequestered in his research facility and making occasional overseas trips to visit foreign tyrants than to the image of the poor, shoeless Socrates causing trouble in the marketplace, refusing to be paid and getting killed by the city for his trouble. But our captivation with this image, once again, is overwhelmingly Plato's invention.

Behind his extraordinary inventiveness, Plato performs a characteristic disappearing trick. Truth to tell, we know very little about Plato. According to Plutarch, he was a lover of figs. Big deal! Plato is mentioned only a couple of times in the many dialogues that bear his name. He was present at Socrates's trial but—in a beautifully reflexive moment that he describes in the *Phaedo*—absent at the moment of Socrates's death because he was sick.

In fact, we don't even know that he was called Plato, which might have been a nickname. Laertius claims that he was called Aristocles, after his grandfather. "Plato" is close to the word "broad" in Greek, like the broad leaves of the *platanos,* or plane tree, under which Socrates and Phaedrus sit and talk about eros. Some think that Plato was so called because his prowess in wrestling had made him broad-shouldered.

I wandered from the Gymnasium across the park and a street to the scant remains of another building in the Academy complex. Approximately 130 feet square, the building's remains have the typical dimensions of a palaestra, or wrestling school. In my mind's eye, I saw an elderly Plato sitting watching his academicians wrestle, occasionally offering coaching advice and encouragement.

Sometimes the less we know, the more space is open to the imagination.

Plato worked at the Academy until his death in 347 BCE, a stay interrupted only by two more extended trips to Sicily. The Academy survived for a few more centuries until it was destroyed by the Roman general Sulla in 87 BCE during the sack of Athens. The buildings were probably burnt along with many other sanctuaries, and the trees from the grove of academe were felled to provide timber for his siege machines. So it goes, I thought.

A faint but clearly perceptible smell of urine hung in the air of the palaestra. At the corner two men were rummaging quietly through a baby-blue refuse bin.

How exposed all these remains were: no fences, no border walls and no security cameras.

It was time to go. On the corner of Hodos Platonos, Plato Street, I noticed a bar unsurprisingly called Platon. I thought about having a quick glass of red wine in Plato's honor but lost courage, took two photos and left.

22

In Aristotle's Garden

February 14, 2019

ATHENS—Aristotle had slender calves. His eyes were small. And he spoke with a lisp, which—according to Plutarch—some imitated. He wore many rings and had a distinctive, rather exotic style of dress: a kind of ancient bling.

I tried to piece together a picture of him as I arrived with my partner at the site of the Lyceum, Aristotle's answer to Plato's Academy, which I had paid a visit to the week before.

Aristotle was reportedly a difficult character—somewhat arrogant, thinking he was cleverer than everyone else (quite possibly true) and even criticizing his master of many years, Plato. He was a perhaps a bit of a *dyskolos,* a grouch, cantankerous, a curmudgeon.

Aristotle was not much loved by the Athenians. This might have been because he was a tricky customer or because he was a *metic:* a resident alien, an ancient green card holder, Greek but decidedly not an Athenian citizen. Given his very close ties to the Macedonian aristocracy, which was extending and tightening its military and political control all across Greece, perhaps the Athenians were right to be suspicious of Aristotle.

We do know that after serving as lector in the Academy and being described as its "Mind" by Plato, Aristotle was not chosen as the latter's successor as scholarch, or head of the school. That job went to Speusippus, Plato's nephew. Aristotle left Athens shortly after Plato's death and stayed away for around twelve years. Was he angry or disappointed not to have been chosen as head of the Academy?

Famously, Aristotle was asked by Philip II of Macedon to be the tutor of his thirteen-year-old son, Alexander. Aristotle set up school in the Macedonian fortress of Mieza and taught the young prince together with his companions, probably around thirty students. A big class. This was a closed school, a boarding school of sorts. A sense of the seriousness with which Aristotle performed his duties can be gleaned from the fact that he composed two treatises in honor of Alexander, "On Kingship" and "On Colonies," as guidebooks for the prince, as well as edited a copy of Homer's *Iliad* specifically for Alexander's use—the "casket copy" (so called presumably because it was kept in a casket).

Very little is known about Aristotle's stay in Macedonia, but it is thought that he was there for quite some time, possibly seven years, and became very friendly with powerful members of Philip's court. In 336 BCE, Philip was assassinated (in a theater, of all places), and Alexander, aged twenty, was declared king. Sensing the instability of political transition, the mighty city of Thebes rebelled against the new Macedonian king. To set an example, Alexander besieged and then wholly incinerated the city, wiping it from the map. Its citizens were either killed or sold into slavery.

Athens didn't make the same mistake; it meekly submitted to the Macedonian pike. Aristotle returned to the city, aged around fifty, in this context. And he came back big time. Because of his metic status, Aristotle was not allowed to buy property.

So—as one does—he rented. He took over a gymnasium site sacred to Apollo Lyceus (the wolf-god) and transformed it into the most powerful and well-endowed school in the world.

Two things hit you when you visit the site of the Lyceum and look at its architectural plans. First, it is a direct copy of Plato's Academy. And second, it is much, much bigger. The relation between the Academy and the Lyceum is a little like that between a twee medieval Cambridge college and the monumental architecture of the University of Chicago.

The reason Aristotle was able to do this was simple: money. If Plato was rich, then Aristotle was wealthier than Croesus, right up there with the Jeff Bezoses of his day. He received the sum of eight hundred talents from his presumably grateful former student, Alexander, which is a vast amount of money (consider that the Plato's Academy cost about twenty-five to thirty talents).

Expressing ancient money values in modern terms presents a perennial puzzle for historians of economics, so I called my colleague, the economist Duncan Foley, for help. He very roughly calculated that the annual GDP of classical Athens was about 4,400 talents. If that is right, 800 talents is a vast amount, equivalent to a fifth or so of the value of all of the city's production. Duncan is somewhat skeptical of the figure. Ancient sources for for numerical data (like the size of armies) are notoriously inaccurate, so perhaps a excited copyist simply added a zero.

Whatever the truth of the matter, Aristotle's immense endowment allowed him to build a huge research and teaching facility and amass the largest and most important library in the world. During the time of Theophrastus, Aristotle's successor as scholarch and evidently a very effective college president, as many as two thousand pupils attended the Lyceum, some of them sleeping in dormitories. The Lyceum was clearly the place to be, the aspirational school destination of choice for the elites. The awkward proximity of philosophy and political power leads one to ponder. Whether the school charged fees is unclear, but given its vast wealth, it probably didn't need to. It sounds a little like Harvard, doesn't it?

The Lyceum was undoubtedly the intellectual projection of Macedonian political and military hegemony. In 323 BCE, when news of Alexander the Great's death in Babylon at the age of thirty-two reached Athens, simmering anti-Macedonian sentiment spilled over, and the popular Athenian leader Demosthenes was recalled. Aristotle left the city for the last time in fear of his life, after a little more than a decade in charge of the Lyceum. Seeing himself justly or unjustly in the mirror of Socrates and fearing charges of impiety, Aristotle reportedly said, "I will not allow the Athenians to sin twice against philosophy." He withdrew to his late mother's estate at Chalcis on the island of Euboea and died there shortly afterward, of an unspecified illness, at sixty-three.

Looking now at the beautifully maintained site of the Lyceum, which is comparatively new by Athenian standards, for excavations didn't begin until 1996, and it was opened to the public in 2014, we are only now beginning to form a proper picture of the plan, architecture and function of the Lyceum. A book detailing our knowledge of Aristotle's school, by archaeologist Efi Lygouri-Tolia and our constant companion Mr. Staikos, is currently being prepared for publication.

As I wandered around the ruins, it was something else that caught my eye and tickled my fancy: the garden. The Lyceum, in its northwest corner, had a garden, which possibly led to the *peripatos,* or shaded walk, from which the promenading Peripatetic school derived its name. Indeed, there were gardens in all the earlier philosophical schools, in the schools of Miletus on the present-day Turkish coast and allegedly in the Pythagorean schools in southern Italy. Plato's Academy had a garden. And later, the school of Epicurus was simply called The Garden. Theophrastus, who did so much to organize the library and build up its scientific side, with maps, globes, specimens, and such like, was a keen botanist like Aristotle and eventually retired to his garden, which was close by.

What was the garden for? Was it a space for leisure, strolling and quiet dialectical chitchat? Was it a mini-laboratory for botanical observation and experimentation? Or was it—and I find this the most intriguing possibility—an image of paradise? The ancient Greek word *paradeisos* appears to be borrowed etymologically from Persian, and it is said that Darius the Great had a "paradise garden," with the kinds of flora and fauna with which we are familiar from the elaborate design of carpets and rugs. Sitting on a Persian carpet is like visiting a memory theater of paradise. It is possible that Milesian workers and thinkers had significant contact with the Persian courts at Susa and Persepolis. Maybe the whole ancient Greek philosophical fascination with gardens is a Persian borrowing, an echo of the influence of their vast empire. But who knows?

I am hardly a gardener. In fact, I have always been remarkably insensitive to the pleasures that many green-thumbed folk find in their backyards. Voltaire's advice in *Candide* that "Il faut cultiver notre jardin" (It is necessary to look after our garden) always struck me as ironic, flippant and defeatist. But now I am not so sure. Perhaps there is a much closer relation between gardens and philosophical thought than we might at first imagine. At the end of the *Nicomachian Ethics,* Aristotle sees the promise of philosophy as the cultivation of the contemplative life, the *bios theoretikos,* which would be the equal to the life of the gods. What better place for this than a garden? Might not botany be the royal road to paradise, an activity at once empirical and deeply poetic?

I visited the Lyceum with my partner, who has keener eyes than I. Together we identified thyme, lavender, abundant wild-flowers, gigantic rosemary bushes, olive trees, cypress and possibly oregano. A carpet of moss with varying shades of green was framed by the sandy yellow footings of the ruins. The whole site suddenly seemed to be a vast garden, and one could feel its proximity to the peak of Mount Lycabettus and outward to the mountains that girdle Athens, and the vast open blue sky.

Very low rope barriers separated off areas that visitors were not meant to visit. I looked around for a guard, saw no one, stepped onto the green moss and made my way quietly to the location of Aristotle's library. On my hands and knees, I saw the ground was littered with tiny delicate snail shells, no bigger than a fingernails, scattered like empty scholars' backpacks. My partner gave me one and I put it in my pocket. I had it on my desk right in front of me as I was writing this. Inadvertently, I crushed it to pieces under the weight of one of Mr. Staikos's huge tomes on the history of libraries. There's probably a moral in this, but it escapes me.

23

The Tragedy of Democracy

February 26, 2019

ATHENS—Our next location is a mere one hundred steps from where I'm writing these essays. I pass it every day on my way to and from the library. It is the Monument of Lysicrates, built around 334 BCE, just about the time Aristotle returned to Athens to found his Lyceum. I always pause there to take in the view and watch the many seemingly well-fed and contented cats scattered around the place. If you let your eyes drift up from the monument, your vision is seized by the vast sacred rock of the Acropolis. It is skin-pinchingly sublime.

Indeed, New Yorkers might experience a feeling of déjà vu or double vision with this monument because you can find not one but two copies of it atop the San Remo apartment building on Central Park West, just north of the Dakota, where John Lennon lived and died. The monument was also widely copied elsewhere.

The original Monument of Lysicrates is composed of a limestone foundation nine and a half feet square topped with a thirteen-foot-high cylindrical edifice. There are six Corinthian columns, thought to be the earliest surviving examples of that style, made from marble from Mount Pentelicus, which is about fifteen miles northeast of Athens. These support a sculpture divided into three bands that carry an inscription commemorating Lysicrates—a wealthy patron of the arts of whom little else is known—and a frieze depicting the adventures of the god Dionysus and some pirates whom he transformed into dolphins. The god sits caressing a panther as satyrs serve him wine while others, with torches and clubs, drive the pirates into the sea.

Above the sculpture is a shallow dome that is the base for three rather mutilated scrolls in the shape of acanthus leaves; the scrolls, which stand about three feet high, were designed to hold a large bronze trophy, or *tripod,* which has long since disappeared. To my eyes, what remains resembles a rather lovely large broken flower vase.

What does this monument, with all these elements, mean? And why is it important?

The monument commemorates Lysicrates's triumph in the dramatic contest, or agon, of the world's first theater festival: the City or Great Dionysia, first established in Athens deep in the sixth century BCE. As with theater and opera today, there was patronage of the arts in classical Athens. To be asked to perform a tragedy was, in ancient Greek, to be granted a chorus. Tragedians were sponsored by a choregos, a chorus bringer, a wealthy or important Athenian citizen, who would recruit choristers and pay for everything. Lysicrates was one.

We do not know how tragic poets and choregoi were matched. But the oldest piece of theater that we possess, *The Persians* by Aeschylus from 472 BCE, was sponsored by the young Pericles, the great champion of Athenian democracy. When a tragic tetralogy won (that's three plays plus a satyr play in which the preceding dramas were openly ridiculed), the sponsor and not the playwright was declared the victor, and a memorial or trophy was erected to display the bronze tripod of the winning choregos. The trophies were displayed in the Hodos Tripodon, the Street of the Tripods.

The street still bears this name. It would once have been littered with tripods, but all except for that of Lysicrates have now disappeared. The City Dionysia began with a procession along this street, with all the citizens, foreigners, visiting dignitaries and choregoi dressed in their finery. At the front of the procession a wooden effigy of Dionysus was carried aloft. The Dionysus that was honored at the festival was the patron god of Eleutherae, a village on the border between Attica and the neighboring region of Boeotia. But the place-name also recalls the Greek word for freedom, *eleutheria:* the link between the theater festival and experience of liberation would have been hard to miss.

So, let's liberate our minds for a moment and imagine that you and I could take a walk right now together along the Street of the Tripods. We could follow the road as it extends eastward from the agora of the ancient city and then bends around the southeast corner of the Acropolis. We might pass clusters of slow-moving tourists and groups of schoolchildren, the bars and tavernas vying for custom on a slow winter's afternoon, Lulu's Bakery and Deli, and perhaps stop—in honor of Dionysus, god of the vine and intoxication—for a glass of overpriced and rather routine red wine from Diogenes Patisserie (the locals call the Monument of Lysicrates the Lamp of Diogenes, alluding to the light that the first of the Cynics was reputed to carry in order to try to find an honest man in Athens).

We could set down our glasses, leave the patisserie, make a sharp right and ascend the steep steps of the narrow Hodos Epimenidou, named after Epimenides, source of the famous liar paradox. We might see a pair of young lovers lost in an embrace and two old gentlemen distractedly gambling with scratch cards. But then, at the top of the steps, we would find ourselves directly facing the sweeping south slope of the Acropolis. Spreading out before us is the Theater of Dionysus. It was here, and nowhere else, that theater began almost three millennia ago. I find this thought a continuous source of astonishment. It was here that possibly around fourteen thousand people sat in late March or early April each year and watched plays all day, including the thirty-one tragedies by Aeschylus, Sophocles and Euripides that survive.

It is tempting to lose oneself, like the young Nietzsche, in Dionysian revelry. And it is always nice to take a walk. But it is also crucially important to remember that the City Dionysia was one of the key institutions in that astonishing Athenian political invention that Nietzsche detested: democracy. The first reference to a democratic assembly voting procedure occurs in Aeschylus's early tragedy *The Suppliant Maidens*, from 470 BCE.

But ancient tragedy is not just a celebration or vindication of democracy or Athenian glory (although Athens does come off quite well in some of the plays). Rather, theater is the place where the tensions, conflicts and ambiguities of democratic life are played out in front of the people. It is the place where those excluded from Athenian democracy are presented on stage: foreigners, women and slaves. Theater is the night kitchen of democracy.

Let's return to our monument. In June 2016, the Greek press reported that the Monument of Lysicrates had been daubed with graffiti by "anarchists." The green spray-painted uppercase lettering read, "Your Greek monuments are concentration camps for immigrants." The sentiment was a little extreme, perhaps, but I was intrigued. Although the offending words were quickly removed, when I looked closely in clear sunlight last weekend, the words were still partly legible.

Rather than be outraged, I suggest we think about these words. If ancient monuments serve some ideology of Hellenism that is identified with the defense of the Greek state against immigrants, Fortress Europe against the infidel hordes, then I think we are misunderstanding something very significant about ancient Athens in general and tragedy in particular.

Consider the Aeschylus play I mentioned, *The Suppliant Maidens*. The plot is simple: A group of fifty women from Egypt seek refuge in Argos in Greece to avoid being forced into marriage to an equal number of young Egyptian men. The women, called the Danaids, claim refuge on the basis of their ethnicity, their bloodline, which they insist is Greek.

Their father, Danaus, says to King Theseus, "Everyone is quick to blame the alien / Who bears the brunt of every evil tongue." But Theseus insists that even if the maidens can prove their Greek ancestry, this is entirely irrelevant to whether they can be admitted into the city; admission has to be debated and decided in a democratic vote. In this play, ethnic claims to blood legitimacy are subordinated to democratic procedure and the due process of law.

Questions of refuge, asylum seeking, immigration, sexual violence and the duties of hospitality to the foreigner reverberate across so many of the tragedies. Theater is that political mechanism through which questions of democratic inclusion are ferociously negotiated and where the world of myth collides with law. Think of *Antigone*, a play about rival claims to the meaning of law, *nomos*. Or the *Oresteia* trilogy, whose theme is the nature of justice and which even ends up in a law court on the Areopagus, the Hill of Ares, just next to the Acropolis. Tragedy does not present us with a theory of justice or law but with a dramatic *experience* of justice as conflict and law as contest.

To be sure, classical Athens was a patriarchal, imperialist society based on slaveholding. Yet the figures who are silenced in the public realm are represented in the fictions of the theater, as if the democracy that was denied to those figures publicly were somehow extended to them theatrically. As the classicist Edith Hall rightly writes, tragedy is polyphonic: it both legitimizes the chauvinism of Athenian power and glory and gives voice to that which undermines it.

If we fail to understand the polyphony of antiquity, we also might be tempted to pick up a can of spray paint and begin daubing monuments with graffiti.

24

What Really Happened
at Eleusis?

March 12, 2019

ATHENS—It was time to take a journey into the Underworld.

Long before I arrived here in January, I was curious about the Eleusinian Mysteries, the most important ritual in ancient Athens, whose fame spread around the ancient world. What is so intriguing about Eleusis is that not a single one of the many thousands of initiates who took part in the ritual over many centuries ever divulged the secrets of what took place. That's surprising because the ancient city was, to say the least, a chatty place—everything seems to have been up for discussion, dissection, polemic and comic ridicule.

One reason for the silence is obvious: speaking about the ritual was a crime punishable by death. There is a story that the dramatist Aeschylus was prosecuted for revealing truths about the Mysteries in his plays but was found innocent. Alcibiades, Socrates's beloved student and double-crossing political opportunist, is said to have played out scenes from the Mysteries in his home in Athens. But we, in fact, know little.

So what really happened at Eleusis? I set off to find out.

My good friend Nadja Agyropoulou arranged for the chief archaeologist of the site, Kalliope Papangeli, known as Poppy, to be our guide. Poppy has has been working at Eleusis for over thirty years out of sheer love for the place.

We drove there. Snow capped the Penteli mountains to the east. Ahead, the area around the modern town of Elefsina (Eleusis is pronounced Elefsis in Greek) came into view, a sprawling maze including the largest oil refinery in Greece and the rather gothic-looking remains of disused industrial buildings.

In the nineteenth and early twentieth centuries, Elefsina was a major industrial port. Ancient past and modern industrial history collide there awkwardly, as is apparent in the names of many of the factories: the Kronos alcohol production plant, the Isis paint and polish factory, the Heracles and Titan cement companies. (Titan Cement is still in business, and its tall chimneys closely surround the sanctuary.) There are wonderful photographs from 1955 by the Greek surrealist Andreas Embirikos that capture this counterpoint of antiquity and industry. Even today the town is expressive of what the Nobel Prize–winning Greek poet George Seferis called "the ancient monuments and the modern sadness."

We arrived at the site and met in a cafe close to the entrance. The place was packed with locals, and the air was thick with the aroma of coffee and enough lush cigarette smoke to make a New Yorker nostalgic. When the cafe was built, the proprietors asked Poppy what it should be called. She suggested Kykeon, after the name of the drink given to initiates before the Mysteries began. They drank it after three days of fasting and a night of ritual dancing. The drink has been the subject of much fevered speculation. It is widely believed *kykeon* had hallucinogenic effects, similar to those of LSD, because of the presence of ergot, a potentially psychoactive ingredient.

So, were the initiates tripping during the Mysteries? I put the question in a couple of different ways to Poppy, hoping for something a little racy. But she was very clear. Kykeon was composed of barley, mint and water. Nothing more.

Psychedelic, ecstatic and orgiastic fantasies abound everywhere in the discussion of the Mysteries. In Poppy's view, wanting to believe such things says a lot more about us than it does about antiquity. Whatever took place in the Mysteries, it was an enormously powerful experience, the effects of which appear to have lasted a lifetime.

We entered the sanctuary.

The Homeric *Hymn to Demeter*, which is the basis for the myth that shapes the Mysteries, speaks of "the stronghold of fragrant Eleusis." It is perhaps harder to detect that fragrance today, but something very special still hangs in the air.

Around us were several large, well-fed and kind-eyed dogs. "They are psychopomps," Poppy said, "who will lead you to the Underworld." It was here, before the Greater Propylaea, the monumental entrance to the sanctuary, that the initiates would have gathered in the ancient month of Boedromion (roughly September) to take part in the climax of the nine-day festival of the Greater Mysteries.

They would have walked in slow procession from Athens. Led by a priestess of Demeter, holding unknown sacred objects in a casket, there would have been ritual bathing, much singing of songs and hymns, and frequent stops at altars to pour libations and make sacrifices.

Eleusis was an egalitarian ritual. In its heyday, up to three thousand initiates could be received at a time. And anyone could participate: men, women, slaves and even children. There were two conditions of entry: first, each initiate had to understand

Greek. Not to *be* Greek— foreigners took part—but to understand the language in order to grasp what was said during the rituals. Second, initiates could not be guilty of homicide. There could be no blood on the hands of the initiates.

Participation was not required, as it is with religious confirmation. It was, Poppy said, a personal choice that could be made whenever one wished. Nor did participation have to be repeated annually, as with Passover or Easter.

But what happened here? Did Poppy know the secret? And would she tell me?

The background story is simple. Demeter and Persephone. Mother and daughter. An only daughter lost, abducted, and her mother searches desperately for nine days. We sense the mother's sadness. After a long and fruitless search, she sits by a rock in Eleusis and weeps.

Eventually Demeter forces Zeus—the top god—to intervene. Persephone returns from the Underworld, where she had been taken by Pluto. The twist in the tale is that Pluto tricked Persephone into eating a handful of pomegranate seeds, which obliges her to return for a part of each year to the darkness of the Underworld.

Thus, darkness and light, fall and spring, winter and summer. The myth tells of the return of the daughter to her mother and with it the passage from death to life.

Poppy tells me that she is particularly proud to be associated with Eleusis because it is the most feminist of ancient myths. Demeter—a woman—persuaded Zeus to change his mind after originally sanctioning Pluto's abduction of Persephone. Whatever exactly took place during the Mysteries, at its core are a pair of female deities outmaneuvering their apparently more powerful male counterparts.

Initiates for the Mysteries, their stomachs empty apart from the ritual drink of kykeon, would have moved slowly through the long entrance halls of the sanctuary before looking up to their right and seeing a large cave beneath the acropolis. Here was the entrance to Hades. It was called the Plutoneion. An explosive place.

At this point, a remarkable thing would happen. To the side of the Plutoneion is a fake well, cylindrical and extending down into the darkness. It even has little steps down into it cut into the rock. It is out of this shaft that someone playing the role of Persephone—presumably a priestess—would have emerged before the crowd of initiates. She would have walked a few steps from the mouth of the well to a broad round hole in the wall of the cave. Her face and upper body would have been visible, peeping out to the crowd.

At the core of the ritual is the reenactment of the return of Persephone from Hades. Since the Mysteries took place at night, and the only light was cast from torches, the dramatic effect of ritual is not hard to imagine. Indeed, the entire layout of Eleusis is extremely theatrical, with exquisite scenography. Taking the path of the initiates is like moving through stages in all senses of the word. The site is a series of immersive performance spaces where the atmosphere of anticipation relentlessly builds. The Eleusinian priests, called hierophants, taken from only two local families, knew how to build tension and induce in the initiates a feeling of awe. Anyone who does not feel a little awe at Eleusis is missing something.

From the cave, the initiates ascended once again, moving toward the Telesterion, the most important edifice at Eleusis, where the central drama of the Mysteries took place. The great hall is a huge space that had a forest of forty-two high columns supporting a sumptuous coffered ceiling. It could hold the thousands of initiates, sitting on steps, eight rows of which survive, carved directly into the mountain rock. It is just like a theater. In the center of the hall stood a smaller, rectangular building called the Anaktoron, built very precisely over a more ancient site that dates back to the Mycenean Bronze Age. The Anaktoron was the holy of holies, where the sacred objects of Demeter were placed. The only people permitted to enter were the hierophants.

From here, the story of the ritual is shrouded in secrecy. We have no idea what happened. If the huge central hall was a theater, then the Anaktoron was the stage at which initiates looked, and the priests were actors. But we do not possess the script. All that we know are three enigmatic words that describe what took place: *dromena, deiknumena, legomena.* Things done, things shown, things said.

But which things? What was done? What was shown? What was said? We do not know.

I wanted to pursue one more clue that I thought might take us to the heart of the Mysteries. The third and highest stage of initiation into the Mysteries, called the *Epopteia,* was reserved only for those who had been through initiation the previous year. We know nothing of what happened, but according to a later Gnostic source, the height of the epoptic mystery was "the ear of wheat harvested in silence."

Wait . . . wheat? Is that it?

Alongside the very human story of a mother and a daughter lies another story, slightly more mundane but even more important. The Greek word for cereals is *dimitriaka.* Demeter becomes Ceres in the Roman pantheon, hence our word for cereals. Demeter gave human beings two gifts: the return to life, personified by Persephone, and the cultivation of grain. The two gifts are obviously linked: it is food that grants the possibility of life. Bread is the very stuff, staff, of life.

Visual depictions of Demeter and Persephone are on sculpted reliefs and tablets, notably the Great Eleusinian Relief from 440–430 BCE. To the right is Persephone, who is carrying what appears to be a torch to light her way in the Underworld. To the left a lofty-looking Demeter gives the gift of grain. They frame a smaller, naked young man identified as the Eleusinian hero, Triptolemos. It is said that Triptolemos invented agriculture and traveled the world teaching human beings how to cultivate grain.

Grain takes us back once again to the story of the abduction of Persephone. Demeter was not just upset that her daughter had been abducted; she was full of righteous wrath. Because of the injustice that had been done to her, Demeter inflicted famine on the land. It was this threat of famine that might have persuaded Zeus to force Pluto to give up her daughter.

Demeter's reward to her initiates was grain, and therefore food, continued agricultural fertility and the possibility of abundance. I think this is the Eleusian secret.

The remains of grain silos can be found at Eleusis. Near the entrance to the main sanctuary was a significantly sized oblong building, built of blue-gray stone, that would have been filled with grain.

Grain is a constant feature of ancient civilizations, back to the oldest human urban settlements, to cities like Ur in Sumeria, founded around 3800 BCE. Temple complexes were also the location for grain stores, where surplus grain was stored so that it might be distributed in hard times. With the possession of that surplus grain, the first and most important kind of wealth, came religious authority and political power. There is a close material connection between temples and food, between religious observance and the most basic ingredients of social and economic life.

After the Mysteries were finished and the dead were honored with libations poured from special vases, the initiates dispersed.

We don't know exactly, but it would seem that they were released from the rigors of the ritual and allowed to return home.

What did they feel? We will never know. But, in Poppy's view, the experience of the Mysteries was one of participation in grief, the grief of a mother for a daughter, and then an experience of joy, with the daughter's return to life. The joy here was not a state of wild Dionysian ecstasy or a psychedelic trance state. It was more of a relief. And the relief was combined with the expectation of a blessing from the goddess. That blessing was the gift of grain, of life. The sense was that life will continue. It will go on. And there is nothing to fear.

I was pleased to learn during our visit that Elefsina was selected as a European Capital of Culture for 2021—the scheme is meant to foster urban regeneration in poorer parts of Europe. Renewal is desperately needed in Greece, not just because of the continued effects of the debt crisis of the past decade, which continues to devastate the lives of ordinary people, but also because of the huge influx of refugees into Greece in recent years. Skaramagas, a large refugee camp, is just a few miles away on Elefsina Bay.

I was reminded that there is no esoteric wisdom here, no secret code that the Mysteries are hiding. The Mysteries are more concerned with life in the here and now, with what sustains it and how life might continue into the future.

25

We Know Socrates's Fate.
What's Ours?

March 19, 2019

ATHENS—Since we began our tour I have tried to take you to some of the less obvious sites around the ancient city, often at the periphery. But now I want to head right to the center of it: the Agora. This was a large public square, humming with human activity—shopping, gossiping, dramatic performances, military and religious processions—and surrounded on all sides by buildings, including many of the key institutions of Athenian democracy.

Excavations since the 1930s have uncovered the Agora, an open green area, about thirty acres sloping down northwest from the rock of the Acropolis. What I most like about it is its feeling of space, the sense of absence that triggers the imagination and allows one to conjure the ruined city in the mind's eye.

The reason for coming here on this particular day was entirely selfish. It was my birthday, and I wanted to return to my favorite site in Athens and visit the ruins of the house of the source of my name: Simon the Cobbler. He also pretended to be a philosopher of sorts.

My partner and I arrived close to the entrance to the Agora as it opened. A railway line, built in 1891, bisects the northern edge of the site, emitting in use a low, pleasant rumble (not the anxiety-inducing squeal of the New York subway). The train line covers the remains of the Altar of the Twelve Gods and runs alongside the Stoa of Attalos, rebuilt in the 1950s, which houses the small and rather lovely Agora Museum. With standard Athenian counterpoint, colonnades of bright white columns abut garish trackside graffiti. The contradictions reach further back: King Attalos of Pergamon was a student of the philosopher Carneades in the second century BCE, and the presumably grateful alumnus gave his university town the gift of a shopping mall; the forty-two shops in the stoa were rented out by the city. Everything was for sale in the Agora.

It was time for a birthday breakfast: Greek yogurt and a big stack of American-style pancakes soaked with honey. A very drunken Englishman (this was about 9 a.m.) sat just ahead of us, smoking a cigarette and holding onto it with some difficulty. He turned around to look at us for a good long while and said to me, "You're serious, aren't you?" Hardly, I thought. He then started into a series of incoherent anti-German, pro-Brexit rants addressed to no one in particular. The waiters seemed puzzled but tolerated him. Sometimes I do miss England.

A group of about a hundred schoolchildren were talking wildly over one another and waiting at the entrance for their bewildered teachers to buy them tickets. We slipped by them and into the site. We were standing on the Panathenaic way, the ancient processional path that led through the Agora and up to the Acropolis.

Early morning rain had given way to cool sunshine. Some trees were just beginning to blossom, and I buried my nose into flowers that seemed to have the scent of honey, although it could have been the remains of breakfast. But Persephone is definitely on her way back from Hades.

In a row running along the west side of the Agora are the footprints of the key institutions of Athenian democracy: the Metroon, the sanctuary for the mother of the gods and the city archive and records office; the Bouleuterion, where the five hundred citizens chosen by lot each year to serve on the council, or *boule,* met every day; and the Tholos, the modest, round headquarters of the fifty-strong executive committee of the council with space for at least some members to stay overnight to deal with any emergencies. Just up from these buildings was the open area of the Pnyx, where the General Assembly, or *ekklesia,* of citizens met every ten days to speak and to decide the law collectively.

Just above, on a small hill, stands the Hephaisteion, the best-preserved Doric temple in Greece and, for me, the most beautiful building in Athens. Though similar to the Parthenon, it is smaller, more complete, and all the more enjoyable for being slightly ignored. On a visit here last summer, we watched a tortoise slowly lumber from view into the darkness of the surrounding bushes at the back of the temple.

The boundaries of the Agora were marked with marble stones about three feet high called *horoi.* These defined the horizon between public and private space, preventing the encroachment of the latter into the former. Two have been recovered, and each is inscribed with the simple phrase *Horos eimi tes agoras,* "I am the boundary of the Agora." I find the pronoun very interesting. It is not the impersonal address of a piece of legislation: "This is the boundary. Trespassers keep out." Rather, the stone itself speaks.

On the south edge of the site, right next to a boundary stone and therefore just outside the Agora, are the excavated ruins of a small building with a plaque that says *Oikia Simonos,* "the house of Simon." Legend has it that this was the home and workshop of Simon the Cobbler, a good friend of Socrates. Socrates supposedly liked to hang out in Simon's workshop and engage in discussions, free from the public glare.

It is ironic that Socrates might have liked to spend time with a cobbler. Socrates was famously shoeless, a habit widely imitated by some of his followers. So, whatever took place in Simon's house, it wasn't selling shoes. Also, as is clear from many of the Platonic dialogues, Socrates genuinely admired people with practical skills. Sadly, he had none himself.

There is some archaeological support for this legend. A number of hobnails were found during excavations, along with bone eyelets used for tying laces or straps. These are on view in the museum, along with the base of a black-glazed cup, or *kylix,* with the name Simonos scratched onto it. Maybe the story has some truth.

So who was Simon?

Diogenes Laertius, that consummate fabricator, gave Simon his own entry in his *Lives and Opinions of Eminent Philosophers,* adding that Phaedo of Elis was the author of a "genuine" dialogue called *Simon.* When Socrates came into his workshop and began to talk, Simon reportedly made notes of all that he could remember. And Laertius claimed that Simon was the first—*before* Plato—to introduce Socratic dialogues as a form of written conversation. Simon had notes of thirty-three of them, described as "leathern," doubtless because of Simon's occupation. Titles include "On Good Eating," "On Greed" and "On Pretentiousness." Apparently, they were unpretentiously short.

Another story connected with Simon assumed significance for a more anarchic school of street philosophers who followed Socrates: the Cynics, or dog philosophers, so called because they were abusively called dogs and then took on the moniker as a badge of honor. It is said that Simon attracted the attention of Pericles, the most powerful leader of Athenian democracy in the classical period. Pericles promised to protect and support Simon if he came to work for him. But Simon refused because he preferred his *parrhesia*, his freedom of speech.

For the Cynics, only those people who achieved self-sufficiency (*autarkeia*) or independence of mind could truly exercise their freedom of speech. For a cobbler-philosopher like Simon to work for a powerful political figure like Pericles would have undermined that independence and compromised his freedom. Simon thus exemplifies the freedom of the Cynics, namely those who chose a life as free as possible from politics and power, who were cosmopolites, citizens of the world, and not subjects of any particular city or state. By tracing their ancestry through Simon, the Cynics could see themselves as being in a direct lineage from Socrates.

Plato famously described Diogenes the Cynic as a "Socrates gone mad." But this madness is testament to a libertarianism that refused the authoritarian picture of society described in Plato's *Republic* and the *Laws*. Unlike Plato and Aristotle, Diogenes did not work for tyrants. Perhaps this is why tyrants loved him. Legend has it that Diogenes was the philosopher most admired by Alexander the Great. When Alexander met Diogenes, he asked him what he wanted. Diogenes famously replied, "I want you to get out of my light."

I have recently been reading an interesting book called *The Tyrant's Writ* by Deborah Tarn Steiner. It is a study on the relation between writing and tyranny in antiquity. We possess the understandable prejudice that literacy and democracy somehow go together, that a literate society is best able to resist oppression. That might be so, but it overlooks the way tyranny and writing are often conjoined—through the writing of laws and decrees but also through coin stamping, huge inscriptions on columns, and the construction of elaborate triumphal arches, not to mention the branding of slaves, all of which dictatorial regimes assert and exert control over.

Ancient historians like Herodotus often associate writing with "barbarian tyrants from the East," notably the Persians. Democracy, in comparison, is much more concerned with speech.

The historians and dramatists of the classical period repeatedly stated that a democracy depends on the ability of citizens to speak freely and declare their will out loud. As Steiner writes, "It is logos and not writing that exists at the heart of democratic Athens's self-definition and the good speaker— not the writer—who keeps popular government on course." Speech is the hallmark of the democrat, and written communication and legislation repeatedly appear in the depiction of the oligarch. Contemporary political parallels are too numerous and obvious to draw, but it might be noted that President Vladimir Putin of Russia is very fond of citing law.

The association between written law and democracy is much more problematic than one might at first imagine. Think here of the debate about the merits and demerits of a written versus an unwritten constitution, the United States versus Britain, for instance. Writing can thus be seen as opposed to liberty, as the very mechanism of enslavement. Real democracy perhaps requires no written constitution. What it needs are hard-won habits of freedom of speech, persuasion, collective decisionmaking and candor.

Of course, the freedom of speech by which Athens defined itself was famously betrayed by Athens itself. Socrates was charged with impiety toward the gods and corruption of the youth and summoned to face those charges in the Royal Stoa, here in the northwest corner of Agora very close to where I am standing.

We know Socrates's fate. What—we might wonder—is ours?

In our virtual Agora, where the boundary stones separating the private from the public have all been removed, where we live in a new and unprecedented tyranny of writing, of text and texting, where cynicism has taken on a whole new troubling set of meanings, how is that fragile parrhesia of the ancients that defines democracy to be cultivated? And how might it be sustained?

26

The Happiest Man I Ever Met

April 3, 2019

What is it like to be a monk? And what does it take to become one?

What exactly does the life of the monk involve? And why might a person choose such a life?

I traveled from Athens to Mount Athos in northeast Greece to see if I could speak to some monks. As it turned out, some of them were quite chatty. My close friend Anthony Papadimitriou had very kindly arranged the trip to the Holy Mountain, as it is called here. We share an abiding interest in monasticism, although neither of us is fully monkish in his habits.

We had been on the road since very early in the morning when we left the port of Ouranopoli, the City of Heaven, in a small white and orange boat with Captain Yorgos. The only way of approaching long rocky peninsula of Mount Athos is by water, and going there requires a special permit. I had it in my hand, stamped with the seal of the Holy Mountain and with four handwritten signatures. Anthony told me that the monks had checked out my credentials and noticed somewhere online that I was described as an atheist, which is not exactly true. But apparently that was better than being Catholic. On my permit, it read "Anglican," which made me smile.

To understand contemporary Greece and what connects it (and fails to connect it) with antiquity, you have to consider the Orthodox Church, which still has considerable ideological power over Greek life, for good or ill. Christianity is the connecting tissue in the body of Hellenism, for it is here that religious traditions and, most importantly, the Greek language were preserved. The spiritual epicenter of Orthodoxy is Mount Athos, an entirely self-governing monastic republic with its own parliament, which I visited. Legally part of the European Union, Athos is an autonomous state with its own jurisdiction, like the Vatican, although the monks would not appreciate that analogy: the Orthodox Church has still not forgotten the Catholic sacking of Constantinople during the Fourth Crusade in 1204!

The monastic tradition on Athos goes back to the ninth century, although the continuous Christian presence is much older. Athonite legend has it that the Virgin Mary traveled to Athos with Saint John the Evangelist and liked it so much that she asked her son to let it be her garden. Happy to oblige his mother, Jesus agreed. And since that time, the only female creatures allowed on Mount Athos are cats, who are abundant in the monasteries. The Mother of God was apparently the only woman to be allowed in her garden.

We were going to spend three days and two nights in the monastery of Simonopetra, or Simon's Rock, founded in the thirteenth century. The fact that I was the namesake of the founder was a recurrent source of amusement to the monks when we were introduced. Simon was a hermit living in a cave, a five-minute walk downhill from the monastery. A few rocky steps inside a tiny chapel took me up to Simon's cell. It was tiny, cold and bare. He had dreamed of a monastery on the rock in front of his cave and then had the audacity to build it. As one monk said to me, this was the world's first skyscraper. An improbable-looking ten-story building is somehow wrapped around a huge rock with the church at its center. It has been burnt down on several occasions, then rebuilt with great effort. Inside is a bewildering array of staircases, a labyrinth that leads down to the monastic library (there is no elevator).

At present, there are sixty-five monks in Simonopetra, mostly Greek but including eight other nationalities; I met a couple of French monks, and there were new arrivals from Lebanon and Syria. On Athos itself, there are around two thousand monks, mostly living communally in coenobitic monasteries, but others live in very small communities called sketes, each with three or four monks. Thirty or so monks continue to live alone as hermits.

"A monk has to hide himself." These are the words of Abbot Eliseus, the leader of Simonopetra, whom we met on a couple of occasions. I asked him about the monastic life and anxiously tried to impress him with my reading of Saint Anthony and the Desert Fathers and my interest in medieval Christian mysticism. He was extremely polite but clearly underwhelmed. "One cannot learn about being a monk from books," he said. "It is not an idea. It is a life that one can live if one is capable of it. But not everyone is able to do it. You might want to be a monk," he continued, "but you will only find out in the practice of living together, doing everything together and owning nothing. When you live with others in the monastery, your true self is revealed. This takes time." "How long?" I asked. "It can be many years as a novice. If someone is capable of monastic life and the discipline it takes, then that is good," he said. "But it is not for everyone, not even for those who feel tempted by it, because it requires deep humility. A person who wants success in the world has to show himself," he said. "That's fine, but a monk has to be hidden from the world." Anthony explained that I was writing essays for *The New York Times*. The abbot nodded ever so slightly. I felt duly chastened.

Much later on my first day in the monastery, I had an encounter where the life of the monk became much clearer to me. It was with Father Ioanikios, who is the happiest person I have ever met in my life. He briefly introduced himself to me and said, "Tomorrow you and I will go around Mount Athos. We will see the chestnut forests. You're from New York?" "Yes," I said. "Ah, New York. I used to live there." And with that he shook my hand warmly and disappeared. He was a handsome and physically fit man, probably in his late sixties, with the clearest eyes, olive skin and a long white beard.

The next day, after getting up for church at 4 a.m. (the service lasted for three and a half hours) and eating a modest lunch around 10:30, Father Ioanikios took me for a ride in his Toyota 4 × 4 (pretty much the only model I saw on Athos) and told me his story.

He was Greek but also an American citizen who had studied mechanical engineering at NYU in the late 1970s, acquiring a master's degree in economics. He used to live on Thirty-second Street between Madison and Fifth Avenues. He got a really good job with Mobil Oil in New Jersey to which he commuted. "Back in those days, I used to drink a little and go out. You know that club that people went to . . ." "Studio 54?" I said. "Yeah, I used to go there all the time." "Did you ever meet Donald Trump?" I asked. "Trump? That guy? Forget it!"

He was set: living in Manhattan in his mid-twenties, single, with a good job and having a ball. But in his bedroom he had a small icon of the Virgin Mary, to which he used to pray before going to sleep, even when he'd had a little too much to drink. Then, in the early 1980s on a trip back to see his family in Greece, he visited Simonopetra because his grandmother's brother had been a monk there. He visited the cell of an old and very sick monk who had known his relative well. Although the monk couldn't speak and could barely move, Ioanikios told me that something happened in that wordless encounter that stayed with him when he went back to New York. "The old monk had such life in his eyes, such love," Ioanikios said. He couldn't get the experience out of his mind.

He returned to the monastery on a second visit and decided to give up his New York life and become a novice. That was in 1984. He became a monk in 1987 and has stayed ever since. When one becomes a monk, there is a second baptism. So Christos became Ioanikios, after a ninth-century Byzantine saint.

Ioanikios is not an intellectual or a theologian. He is a practical man, in charge of some of the business operations of the monastery, construction projects, road repairs and the purchase of gasoline for the 4 × 4s, a procedure he explained in some detail while driving. He talked fondly of a JCB mechanical digger that he had bought and about what kind of concrete was required to fix the road after snow and storm damage during the winter. But he is a person of deep and convincing faith. He told me that he frequently prays in the forest, for he feels comfortable there. "It's the Garden of Eden," he said. Looking out the car window at the forest, mountains and blue sea, I sighed in agreement. When I asked him more closely about his decision to become a monk, he said that when he came to Simonopetra, he felt called by God and had responded to the call. Not all are called by God, and not all that are called respond. But he did.

I wanted to ask Ioanikios about the monks' daily schedule. The first source of disorientation in the monastery is caused by time. Athos follows the old clock of Byzantium, where the day begins and ends at sunset. According to our vulgar, modern time, Matins begin at 4 a.m. and lasts for three and a half hours. But monks get up much earlier, around 1 a.m. He told me that some of younger, keener monks often get up at 11 p.m. in order to extend their devotions. There is at least one hour of Bible reading, one hour of reciting the Jesus Prayer, the Prayer of the Holy Mountain ("Lord Jesus Christ, have mercy on me," repeated rhythmically over and over again), and one hour of prostrations. The number of prostrations depends on age and physical ability; there should be at least 120, but some monks perform up to 2,000. This rather put my Pilates classes into perspective.

After the morning service, monks can nap for two hours. Naps are followed by a short service of thirty minutes, then by lunch, the main meal of the day, at 10:30. Meals in the refectory are taken in silence. One can eat only when Abbot Eliseus rings the gold bell he has beside him. When a second bell rings, it is permitted to drink either water or the sweet red wine from their own vineyards, provided in a sole glass. Meal times are fast, lasting twenty minutes or so; you have to eat quickly. Throughout the meal, a monk reads aloud from a text—during my stay there, something about Julian the Apostate. When the bell rings, everyone stops eating, and the monks file silently out.

After lunch come four hours of work, which often ends with another hour's prayer. After Vespers, which lasts for ninety minutes or so, there is a modest dinner, again eaten in silence, and then two hours' free time before sleep, spent reading or talking with brothers. The cycle repeats, with ritual variations, every day, with no vacations, no breaks, and no Netflix bingeing, until death brings surcease. The cassock that the monks wear under their robes has a skull and crossbones at the bottom to remind them of mortality. As Saint Evagrius says, the monk should always act as if he were going to die tomorrow.

What struck me during my stay at Simonopetra was the constant emphasis on monasticism as a living experience, as an unbroken continuity of tradition. In the case of Athos, that means one thousand years. The rituals have been followed every day without exception in this place. Monasticism is not a theology; it is a way of life. Abbot Eliseus told me that there are two moments of foundation in Greece: for the Acropolis and for Athos. "But one is dead and the other is living," he said. "One is an idea; the other is a living experience."

Toward the end of our road trip, Ioanikios looked at me with his clear eyes and spoke quietly. "It is hard being a monk. Man was made for something else, to make a family. And we have chosen a different life. This is only possible when the energy comes from God." "What is that energy?" I asked. "It is hard to describe, but you could call it grace." He paused. "When you experience it, it's like you have no enemies. You know what Jesus says in the Sermon on the Mount, 'Love your enemies,' and you think that's a crazy thing to say. How can that be? But when you feel that energy, you feel supported, and it feels like the most obvious thing. You feel only joy and happiness." He repeated the word "joy" three times. "For me, this life is hard, but I feel that joy sometimes when I'm singing."

Let me tell you about the singing. For, truth to tell, I heard Ioanikios sing at Vespers before I spoke to him and had remarked on the strength of his voice. I watched him lead his fellow monks for at least eleven hours during my three days in Simonopetra. On either side of the church, groups of about ten monks clustered around a lectern, chanting in a constant movement of call and response from one side of the church to the other. With subtle harmonies and occasional deliberate discord, the voices flowed back and forth, complementing and counter-pointing each other. Nothing was staccato. Everything was movement and overlapping lines. I have listened to recordings of Byzantine chants, indeed by the choir of Simonopetra itself, but they don't even begin to get close to how it felt in the church.

During the service, the faces of some of the monks whom I had seen and talked to were transformed and elevated by song. It is impossible to describe what it was like to be there, but the sheer duration and intensity of the services had a powerful effect. I was in church for about thirteen hours during my stay, including a five-hour vigil for the Virgin Mary on Saturday evening. There is an absolute seriousness to the monks during the services, but none of the usual clerical piousness. There was much coming and going during the service and quite a lot of talking among the monks, which seemed like the most natural thing in the world. Once I had got to know Ioanikios, he came over to me a few times during a break in the singing to ask how I was doing or to tell me what was happening. ("This is the dance of the angels," he said, as the golden candelabra swung back and forth overhead. "All of heaven is dancing.") Then he would go back to his chanting.

Everything felt loose and completely relaxed. Here were participants in a ritual who knew exactly what they were doing. There was no judgment, hushing or disapproval of a heretic like me. Incense with the scent of myrrh hung heavy in the air from the swinging incense burner that functioned like a percussive accompaniment to the chanting. Smell and sound were heady. Anthony and I were only a few feet away from some of the monks as they sang. There were no sermons and no attempts at contemporary relevance. Everything was song.

I have never seen a church seem so alive. At certain points in the divine liturgy on Sunday, the whole church glowed gold inside as the morning sunlight began to come in. The physical discipline of the monks was hard to comprehend. They stood for hours on end without moving, twitching, fidgeting or biting their nails. No one drank anything or looked thirsty. At other times, all the candles were extinguished, and a low droning chant filled the darkness. Toward the end of the five-hour vigil, around midnight, I noticed one or two stifled yawns, but nothing much. By this time, the monks had been awake for at least twenty-four hours. At the end Ioanikios looked as fresh as a daisy. I was shattered, hungry and thirsty (I hadn't eaten since the previous morning and had had only a few hours' sleep). But I felt such a lightness.

Before we left Athos, Ioanikios showed me his office in a ramshackle building at the tiny port of Daphne. He has dreams of transforming it into a spiritual center for pilgrims. He gave Anthony and me small, hand-carved wooden crosses and placed them around our necks. He also gave me some prayer beads and told me to repeat the Jesus prayer. He said it would help dispel any worries I had in my mind: "Lord Jesus Christ, have mercy on me." He repeated the words. "Keep saying the words, and your cares will disappear."

"Don't forget us," he added in leaving. "And come back every year. You are our friend now."

I took off the cross after returning to Athens late in the evening. I was back in the profane world. And back with my stupid philosophical distance and intellectual arrogance. My time in Athos was the closest to a religious experience that I have ever come. I wonder if I will ever get so close again.

27

An Offering to the Soccer Gods

April 15, 2019

ATHENS—It is about time I told you what I have *really* been doing here the past few months. It hasn't all been visits to archaeological sites and meditations on the contemporary relevance of antiquity. Today I'd like to put ancient history on hold for a moment and move from the past right into the present.

In each essay written in Athens I have focused on a specific material object—offering close observation of a place, a location, a site—and leaned on that object as a lever to open up a story that allows a larger picture of Athens to come into what I hope is a novel focus. I've been trying to build a personal memory theater of this city, a cabinet of treasures and curiosities.

It might be objected that what I have been writing is a series of postcards, perhaps with lots of local color and historical background, but nonetheless a kind of high-end philosophical tourism of famous Athenian locations. Perhaps such a view can't be avoided. I am, after all, a foreigner and a temporary resident. And this city's monuments, with their beauty and historical grandeur, exert a pull like virtually no others. Is there a better way of connecting with ordinary Athenians, with their habits and routines? Maybe I could get closer to their lives in the vast modern Agora of this metropolis through a common passion. A passion for soccer. And what site could be more ordinary than a pub?

I am a lifelong fan of Liverpool Football Club and spend much more time than I care to confess watching games, reading about soccer, listening to podcasts and watching endless YouTube clips of highlights, press conferences and often rather tedious match analyses. I will talk to any poor soul I can find about my team and about theirs, although I prefer mine. Yet—much to my constant amazement—there exist people in the world who do not care for the beautiful game.

The Liverpool team was playing the day after I arrived in Athens in early January. I urgently needed to find out how to watch live games, which was not possible on the TV in my apartment. On the morning of match day, I dipped into the internet and discovered a promising-looking Facebook page for the Pan-Hellenic Liverpool Friends Club. I sent a message, more in hope than expectation.

Three minutes later, I got a reply, saying, "Good morning m8. You can meet us in the Wee Dram pub. It is a Scottish pub. Ask for John."

I arrived early and asked for John. It was like meeting a long-lost friend. John Skotidas founded the official Liverpool supporters club in 1995 and has been running it ever since with a good deal of organizational skill. It boasts eleven hundred members; Liverpool is the most popular English team in Greece. I've grown to know John quite well while I have been here. He was an aircraft engineer with the Greek air force for twenty-seven years before retiring at the age of forty-six to pursue his other passion, watching and talking about soccer. John even has his own YouTube channel. He became a Liverpool fan after seeing the Beatles on TV when he was a kid in the late 1960s. He just liked the name Liverpool: it sounded good. When he was ten years old, he watched the team play for the first time against Newcastle United in the FA Cup final in 1974 and decided to support them. He's been a fan ever since.

I met a number of other people in the bar that first day: Scotty, Kris, Spiros (who promotes Bollywood movies in Greece, which are apparently popular), and a bunch of other Greek fans. I watched my first game with them on January 12, Liverpool versus Brighton. It was an edgy match, but with a confident defensive display from us, we won 1–0.

Since then, I've watched a lot of games at the Wee Dram, and a ritual of sorts has developed. I have a talked a fair bit about the nature of ritual in these Athens essays, whether the processional pomp of the City Dionysia, the divine liturgy of Mount Athos, or the Greater Mysteries of Eleusis. Watching soccer is a lesser mystery, with a more humble and humdrum set of ritual actions, but its rituals also have meaning. Every fan has rituals and superstitions.

Before leaving the apartment, I select my Liverpool shirt, tracksuit or scarf (depending on the weather, but I always look a teensy bit ridiculous) and walk to Syntagma, Constitution Square. I descend into the underworld of the subway system, take the four stops to Panormou station, buy a piece of spana-kopita, a sumptuous spinach pie, from the bakery, walk slowly uphill eating it, get to the Wee Dram, push open the door, scan the room for seats and look for John. He's always sitting in the same spot (it's a superstition, he told me), just next to the big TV, head down, looking at his phone. Although I try and get there early, the place is usually packed. John seems to have a secret supply of stools that he can whip out if a regular comes in late and the place is crammed with fans.

John gives the nod, says a few words, and a seat opens up. I shake hands with everyone, ask them how they are doing, head to the bar, buy a pint of Murphy's (no Guinness is sold), sit down, and check the WhatsApp connection with my son Edward in London. We exchange a couple of short messages like "I'm in position. You?" and discuss the team lineup, usually wondering why our German coach, Juergen Klopp, has included or left out a player we particularly like. The Wi-Fi tends to keep dropping, which occasions much dashing out into the street.

The Wee Dram is owned by Ross, who used to play for the Scottish national basketball team (I didn't know Scotland had one) and supports Heart of Midlothian. To each his or her own. The pub has two main areas, a glass-walled central room where you can buy drinks, which is where the younger lads tend to gather, standing together in small groups, often wearing Liverpool shirts, and a larger outside area with older fans, sitting or standing. I prefer to sit, at least until something exciting happens, and then I stand and retreat backwards to the door of the pub so I don't block anyone's view. For reasons that completely escape me, I often crouch with my arms at a right angle and my fists softly clenched. It's almost an attitude of prayer.

At a large wooden central rectangular table with benches is where the hardcore fans sit, with John in pole position, top left. Most of them are smoking (Athens is a great place to pick up a passive smoking habit. Smoking is banned, but Greeks tend to do what they want), drinking beer or coffee and betting online on their phones. Just behind the central table is another, smaller table with four or five seats marked "reserved" (although it turns that all the tables are "reserved"). This is where I sit, usually with some familiar faces. We talk to each other as much as we can in broken English and fragmentary Greek, going into great detail about the qualities of particular players, tactics, formations and the strength of the opposition. Although we don't know each other well, there is an immense of feeling of familiarity, affection and trust.

To the non-fan, it's hard to explain how detailed these discussions are and the extraordinary levels of knowledge that ordinary fans possess. There is, in fact, an amazing rational intelligence to soccer talk, subtended by a common passion for the team that we all love.

The teams emerge, I sit up straight, and the usual fluff of TV commercials and dumb graphics take the screen before kickoff. We all clap when the whistle blows, and then we enter the shared and strangely meditative flow of the game. The pub gets really quiet. There is always an odd experience of tension in watching a game with a group of fellow fans while waiting for your team to score or at least have a shot or engage in a compelling passage of play. The TV in the Wee Dram has useless speakers, so catching the Greek commentary is a strain. Not really understanding the words, I listen eagerly for the names, which have an almost magical aura: Van Dijk, Robertson, Sadio Mané, Milner, Alexander-Arnold.

Complaints abound when there is a misplaced pass or especially when our star forward player, Mohamed Salah, shoots and misses, which has been happening a lot of late. The most frequently heard word in the bar is *malakas*. Let's just say this is a word with a wide range of semantic connotations, many of them connected with the sin of onanism. The connection between soccer and swearing is visceral. I am at my most disgustingly foul-mouthed when watching Liverpool play, a fact of which I am not proud. I often try and swallow the vowel after the first consonant of the bad word has spilled from my lips.

When we score, the place explodes. Skintight anxiety suddenly releases into ecstasy. Everyone leaps up; there are wild scenes of joy, hugging and loud cries. I high-five everyone around the table, why I don't know. It's not my style. But I started the habit at my first Wee Dram match in January and somehow feel obliged to continue.

When the opposing team scores, there is absolute silence in the bar. Not a word. Barely any reaction. The mood shifts entirely, and no one speaks for at least ten seconds, then: "malakas."

My three months in Athens has been a very tense time to be a Liverpool fan. A six-point January lead in the English Premier League has been whittled away by the relentlessness of our main opponents and the reigning champions, Manchester City, and by Liverpool's drawing a number of games that we should have won. We've lost some of our flair, flow and attacking rhythm. But we're still in there fighting, match by match, grinding out victories, often with last-minute goals. Watching is a nerve-shredding experience.

Today, March 31, features an absolutely vital game. I arrive very early at the Wee Dram, about forty-five minutes before kickoff, around 5:45 p.m. There is a lot of banter, more beer is being drunk than usual, and servers slide through the crowd setting down pizzas, which are always shared. Liverpool is playing Tottenham Hotspur, and my son Edward is at the Anfield Road stadium with his mate Ben watching live. A large part of the reason why the fate of Liverpool Football Club in this season's English Premier League matters so much to me is because of him. I deviously programmed him in his childhood years to support Liverpool, and he is now a more knowledgeable fan than I. But he has never seen Liverpool win the league; it is twenty-nine years since that last happened. Liverpool won thirteen times during my first thirty years on planet earth. But that history feels as ancient as Athens itself.

Spurs is a fine team. Some of my best friends are Spurs fans. They didn't deserve to lose that day. But, very obligingly, they did, thanks to a goalkeeping blunder from World Cup–winning French captain Hugo Lloris off a cheeky header from the sinuous Salah, which ricocheted into the net off the shin of Toby Alderweireld in the ninetieth minute of the match. Call it luck, if you like. I choose to call it destiny.

It is hard to describe the feeling of sheer unconfined joy when your team wins. Everything is right with the world, and the mind is free of any concern or gnawing introspection. Here at the Wee Dram, fans share a genuine feeling of warmth and solidarity. Despite the linguistic limitations, we understand each other very well because we have a team in common. Indeed, there are three hundred official Liverpool supporters clubs all around the world and countless other millions watching in whatever way they can. After the Spurs game, Ross played the Liverpool anthem, "You'll Never Walk Alone" by Gerry and the Pacemakers, and everyone sang along, bellowing out of tune at the top of their voices.

I realize that such rituals are shallow and far too sentimental, but at such moments I feel a real sense of disinhibited belonging, and other people feel the same. To quote the current club mantra: "We are Liverpool. This means more."

After the song climaxed and the final chorus faded, I finished my beer and looked for John to say good-bye. He'd already left.

Will we win the league? Probably not. Manchester City is a better football team. But today we won. I don't so much walk as glide down the hill to the subway station, texting with Edward and reading the early match reports. I pick up a loaf of bread at the bakery and head back into the center of the city. Life is good.

Others

28

There Is No Theory of Everything

September 12, 2015

Over the years, I have had the good fortune to teach a lot of graduate students, mostly in philosophy, and have noticed a recurring fact. Behind every new graduate student stands an undergraduate teacher. This teacher was someone who opened the student's eyes and ears to the possibility of the life of the mind, a possibility that the student had perhaps imagined but scarcely believed was within reach. Someone who, through the force of example, animated a desire to read more, study more and know more. Someone with whom the student discovered something fascinating or funny or downright strange. Someone who heard something significant in what the student said and gave the student confidence and self-belief. Such teachers are the often unknown and usually unacknowledged (and under-paid) heroes of the world of higher education.

Some lucky people have several such teachers. I did. But there is usually one teacher who sticks out and stays in one's mind, whose words resound down through the years. Such teachers feature in all sorts of anecdotes and are fondly recalled through multiple bon mots and jokes told by their former students. Very often, too, really good teachers don't write or don't write that much. They are not engaged in "research," whatever that benighted term means with respect to the humanities. They teach. They talk. Sometimes they even listen and ask questions.

In relation to philosophy, this phenomenon is hardly new. The activity of philosophy begins with Socrates, who didn't write and about whom many stories were told. Plato and others, like Xenophon, wrote down the stories and we still read them. Often the center of a vivid philosophical culture is held by figures who don't write but who exist mainly through the stories that are told about them. One thinks of Sidney Morgenbesser, longtime philosophy professor at Columbia, whom I once heard described as a "mind on the loose." The philosopher Robert Nozick said of his undergraduate education that he "majored in Sidney Morgenbesser." On his deathbed Morgenbesser is said to have asked: "Why is God making me suffer so much? Just because I don't believe in him?"

These anecdotes seem incidental, but they are very important. They become a way of both revering teachers and humanizing them, both building them up and belittling them, giving us a feeling of intimacy with them, keeping them within human reach. Often the litmus test of an interesting philosopher is how many such stories circulate.

I want to talk here about an undergraduate teacher of mine about whom many stories were told but who is not widely known. Frank Cioffi (1928–2012), an Italian American from a peasant family, spent his early years close to Washington Square. His mother died giving birth to him, and his distraught father died when Frank was an infant. He was brought up by his grandparents, who spoke in a Neapolitan dialect. He dropped out of high school, spent time with the United States Army in Japan and then in France identifying dug-up corpses of American soldiers for the Commonwealth War Graves Commission. In 1950 he somehow managed to get into Ruskin College, Oxford, on the GI Bill; there he began to study philosophy and discovered the work of Wittgenstein, whose later thinking was just then beginning to circulate. In the early 1970s, after teaching in Singapore and Kent, England, he became the founding professor of the philosophy department at the University of Essex. I encountered him there in 1982. The meeting was memorable.

Frank (that is how he was always referred to) has recently become the subject of an interesting book by David Ellis, *Frank Cioffi: The Philosopher in Shirt-Sleeves*. The book gives a very good sense of what it felt like to be in a room with Frank. Truth to tell, Ellis's title is deceptive, for I never recall seeing Frank in shirtsleeves. He wore a sweater, usually inside out. He never had laces in the work boots he always wore, and strangest of all, because of an acute sensitivity to fabrics, he wore pajamas underneath his clothes at all times. The word "disheveled" doesn't begin to describe the visual effect that Frank had on the senses. He was a large, strong-looking man, about six foot four. The pajamas were visible at the edges of his sweater, his fly was often undone (some years later, his only teaching advice to me was "always check your fly") and he sometimes seemed to hold his pants up with a piece of string. In his pockets would be scraps of paper with typewritten quotations from favorite writers like George Eliot and Tolstoy or from Arthur Conan Doyle's Sherlock Holmes, whom he revered.

He walked the few miles to the brutal architectural dystopia that was the University of Essex from his home in Colchester wearing an early version of a Sony Walkman. I assumed he was listening to music, only to discover years later that he was listening to recordings of himself reading out passages from books. I remember him saying during a lecture that he was "not a publishing philosopher." This was not quite true. His books, like *Wittgenstein on Freud and Frazer* (1998), are fascinating, but his rather tangled prose gives no sense of what it was like to listen to one of his lectures. They were amazing, unscripted and hugely funny performances during which he would move about over a vast range of quotations and reflections, his considerable bulk straining to control the passion of his thinking. Occasionally he would perch himself on the edge of a student's desk and sit there smoking a small Indian cigarette (yes, it was that long ago). We were at once terrified and enthralled.

I was studying English and European literature in my first year at college, but my friend Will and I were considering switching to philosophy partly because of Frank. We went to see him in his office for advice. I don't remember his giving any. We sat with him for about an hour, and I remember a story about how, when he was teaching in Singapore, he used to put down poison to deal with the many cockroaches that infested his office. One day, while watching an insect die in agony in the corner of his room, he realized that "there is a problem with other minds after all. It is a real issue." He knew, he said, "that the bug was dying in pain." He "felt profound sympathy and stopped doing it." Will and I both switched to philosophy immediately and never looked back.

Some years later, I went back into his office to ask permission to switch from one course to another. "Which courses?" he asked indifferently. "I'm meant to be reading Foucault, but I want to do a course on Derrida." "Man," he replied, "that's like going from horseshit to bullshit." In fact, as others can confirm, the latter word was his most common term of reference, and it also expressed his approach to philosophy: No BS.

In the preface to *The Varieties of Religious Experience*, William James said that it was his belief that "a large acquaintance with particulars often makes us wiser than the possession of abstract formulas, however deep." This was Frank's pedagogical credo. His teaching moved from particular to particular; he often worked from the quotations written on small slips of paper that he stuck into his pockets and pulled out with great dramatic effect. He hated big theories and any kind of metaphysical pretension, and he would use little quotations to pick away relentlessly at grand explanations. He used the particular to scratch away at the general, like picking at a scab.

Frank's special loathing was reserved for Freud, whom he thought a writer of great perceptiveness and expressive power but completely deluded about the theoretical consequences of his views. "Imagine a world in which, like ours," Frank wrote in *Wittgenstein on Freud and Frazer,* "people laughed at jokes, but unlike ours did not know what they were laughing at until they discovered the unconscious energic processes hypothesized by Freud." For Frank, such was the world that Freud beguiled himself and us into believing we were living in. Frank compared the twentieth-century fascination with psychoanalysis to the nineteenth-century fascination with phrenology, the "science" of bumps on the head. I think he would have come to very similar conclusions about the early twenty-first-century fad for neuroscience and our insatiable obsession with the brain.

Despite the astonishing breadth of his interests, Frank's core obsession in teaching turned on the relation between science and the humanities. More particularly, his concern was with the relation between the causal explanations offered by science and the kinds of humanistic description we find, say, in the novels of Dickens and Dostoevsky and in the sociological writings of Erving Goffman and David Riesman. His quest was to clarify the occasions when a scientific explanation was appropriate and when it was not and we needed instead a humanistic remark. Our confusions about science and the humanities, he was convinced, had wide-ranging and malign societal consequences.

Let me give an example. Imagine that you are depressed because of the death of a loved one or just too much hard and seemingly pointless work. You go to see a doctor. After you explain what ails you, with the doctor fidgeting and looking at the time, the doctor exclaims: "Ah, I see the problem. Take this blue pill and you will be cured." However efficacious the blue pill might be, in this instance the doctor's causal diagnosis is the wrong one. What you need is to be able to talk, to feel that someone understands your problems, and perhaps to be offered some insight or even suggestions on how you might move forward in your life. This, one imagines, is why people go into therapy.

But let's flip it around. Let's imagine that you are on a ferry crossing the English Channel during a severe winter storm. Your nausea is uncontrollable, and you run out onto the deck to vomit the contents of your lunch, breakfast and the previous evening's dinner. You feel so wretched that you no longer fear death—you wish you were dead. Suddenly, on the storm-tossed deck, R. D. Laing appears. The most skilled, charismatic and rhetorically gifted existential psychiatrist of his generation, standing there in a blue velvet suit, proceeds to give you an intense phenomenological description of how your guts feel, the sense of disorientation, the corpselike coldness of your flesh, the loss of the will to live. This response to your ill health is also an error. On a ferry you want a blue pill that is going to alleviate the symptoms of seasickness.

Frank's point is that our society is deeply confused about the occasions when a blue pill is required and not required, when we need a causal explanation and when we need a further description, clarification or elucidation. We tend to get muddled and imagine that one kind of explanation (usually the causal one) is appropriate on all occasions.

What is in play here is the classical distinction made by Max Weber between explanation and clarification, between causal or causal-sounding hypotheses and interpretation. Weber's idea is that natural phenomena require causal explanation, of the kind given by physics, say, whereas social phenomena require elucidation—rich, expressive descriptions. In Frank's view, one major task of philosophy is to help us get clear on this distinction and to provide the right response at the right time. This, of course, requires judgment, which is no easy thing to teach.

Let me push this idea a little further. At the end of his book on Wittgenstein, Frank tells a story about a philosophical paper (imagined or real, it is not clear)* with the title "Qualia and Materialism: Closing the Explanatory Gap." The premise of the paper is twofold: first, there is a gap between how we experience the world—our subjective, conscious experiences (qualia)—and the scientific explanation of the material forces that constitute nature; and, second, the gap can potentially be closed with one overarching theoretical explanation. Frank points out that if we can imagine such a paper, we can also imagine papers called "The Big Bang and Me—Closing the Explanatory Gap" or "Natural Selection and Me—Closing the Explanatory Gap."

This is the risk of what some call scientism—the belief that natural science can explain everything, right down to the details of our subjective and social lives. All we need is a better form of science, a more complete theory, a theory of everything. Lord knows, there are even Oscar-winning Hollywood movies

---

* Actually, the paper exists. I know this because its author, Clyde L. Hardin, kindly emailed me after my essay appeared in *The New York Times*. It can be found in *Philosophy and Phenomenological Research*, vol. 48, no. 2 (December 1987): 281–98.

made about this topic. Frank's point, which is still hugely important, is that there is no theory of everything, nor should there be. There is a gap between nature and society. The mistake, for which scientism is the name, is the belief that this gap can or should be filled.

Scientism invites, as an almost allergic reaction, the total rejection of science. As we know to our cost, we witness this every day with climate-change deniers, flat-earthers and religious fundamentalists. Obscurantism is the name for this response, namely that the way things are explained is not by science but with reference to occult forces like God, all-conquering Zeus, the benign earth goddess or fairies at the bottom of the garden. To confront the challenge of obscurantism, we do not need to run into the arms of scientism. What is needed is a clear overview of the occasions when a scientific remark is appropriate and when something else is required—the kind of elucidation we find in stories, say, or poetry or indeed a movie or good TV (Frank watched a lot of TV).

People often wonder why there appears to be no progress in philosophy, unlike in natural science, and why it is that after three millennia of philosophical activity no dramatic changes seem to have been made to the questions philosophers ask. The reason is that people keep asking the same questions and keep getting perplexed by the same difficulties. Wittgenstein puts the point directly: "Philosophy hasn't made any progress? If somebody scratches the spot where he has an itch, do we have to see some progress?" Philosophy scratches at the various itches we have, not so we might find a cure for what ails us but so we can scratch in the right place and begin to understand why we itch. Philosophy is not Neosporin. It is not a healing balm. It is the opposite, an irritant, which is why Socrates described himself as a gadfly.

Thinking of philosophy as an irritant is one way of approaching the question of life's meaning. Human beings have been asking the same kinds of questions for as long as there have been human beings to ask. It is not an error to ask. It testifies to the fact that human beings are rightly perplexed by their lives. The mistake is to believe that there is an answer to the question of life's meaning. As Douglas Adams established quite some time ago, the answer to the question of life, the universe and everything will always be "42" or some variation thereof. In other words, the answer will be rather disappointing.

The point, then, is not to seek an answer to the meaning of life but to continue to ask the question. This is what Frank did in his life and teaching. David Ellis tells a story of when Frank was in the hospital and a friend came to visit him. When the friend could not find Frank's room, he asked a nurse where he might find Professor Cioffi. "Oh," the nurse replied, "you mean the patient that knows all the answers." At which point, a voice was heard from under some nearby bedclothes. "No, I know all the questions."

We don't need an answer to the question of life's meaning, just as we don't need a theory of everything. What we need are multifarious descriptions of many things, further descriptions of phenomena that change the aspect under which they are seen, that light them up and let us see them anew. That is what Frank was doing with his quotations, with his rich variety of particulars. They allow us to momentarily clarify and focus the bewilderment that is often what passes for our "inner life"; they give us an overview. We might feel refreshed and illuminated, even slightly transformed, after a moment of clarification, but we aren't going to stop scratching that itch. In 1948, Wittgenstein wrote, "When you are philosophizing you have to descend into primeval chaos and feel at home there."

Allow me an odd postscript. Shortly after I learned the news of Frank's death in 2012, I opened my email one morning to find a message from "Frank Cioffi." I paused, as if someone had walked over my grave or scratched my skin with their nails, only to discover that his namesake was Frank's nephew, a professor of English at City University of New York, who was doing research into his uncle's work. That's the great thing about one's teachers. They never really die. They live on in the stories we tell about them.

29

The Dangers of Certainty
A Lesson from Auschwitz

February 2, 2014

As a kid in England, I watched a lot of television. There weren't any books in our house, not even the Bible. TV was therefore pretty important, even omnipresent. Most of what it delivered was garbage. But in 1973, the BBC aired an extraordinary documentary series called *The Ascent of Man,* hosted by one Dr. Jacob Bronowski, with thirteen hour-long episodes. Each episode was what he called an essay and involved exotic and elaborate locations, but the presentation was never flashy and consisted mostly of Dr. Bronowski speaking directly and deliberately to the camera.

Dr. Bronowski (he was always referred to as "Dr." and I can't think of him with a more familiar moniker) died forty-one years ago this year, at the relatively young age of sixty-six. He was a Polish-born British mathematician who wrote a number of highly regarded books on science but who was equally at home in the world of literature. He wrote his own poetry as well as a book on William Blake.

He was a slight, lively, lovely man. Because it was the early 1970s, some of his fashion choices were bewilderingly pastel, especially his socks, although on some occasions he sported a racy leather box jacket. He often smiled as he spoke, not out of conceit or because he lived in California (which, incidentally, he did, working at the Salk Institute in San Diego), but out of a sheer, greedy joy at explaining what he thought was important. A genuine humility in his demeanor made him utterly likeable.

The Ascent of Man (admittedly a little sexist now—great men abound, but there are apparently a few great women too!) deliberately inverted the title of Darwin's 1871 book. It was an account, not of human biological evolution, but of cultural evolution—from the origins of human life in the Rift Valley of Africa to the shifts from hunter-gatherer societies to nomadism, settlement and civilization, from agriculture and metallurgy to the rise and fall of empires: Assyria, Egypt, Rome.

Bronowski presented everything with gusto and with a depth that never sacrificed clarity and was never condescending. The tone of the programs was rigorous yet permissive, playful yet precise, and always urgent, open and exploratory. I remember in particular the programs on the trial of Galileo, Darwin's hesitancy about publishing his theory of evolution and the dizzying consequences of Einstein's theory of relativity. Some of it was difficult for a thirteen-year-old to understand, but I remember being riveted.

The ascent of man was secured through scientific creativity. But unlike many of his more glossy and glib contemporary epigones, Dr. Bronowski was never reductive in his commitment to science. Scientific activity was always linked to artistic creation. For Bronowski, science and art were two neighboring mighty rivers that flowed from a common source: the human imagination. Newton and Shakespeare, Darwin and Coleridge,

Einstein and Braque: all represented interdependent facets of the human mind and what was best and most noble about the human adventure.

For most of the series, Dr. Bronowski's account of human development was a relentlessly optimistic one. Then, in the eleventh episode, "Knowledge or Certainty," the mood changed to somber. Let me try and recount what has stuck in my memory for all these years.

He began the show with the words "One aim of the physical sciences has been to give an actual picture of the material world. One achievement of physics in the twentieth century has been to show that such an aim is unattainable." For Dr. Bronowski, there was no absolute knowledge, and anyone who claims it—whether a scientist, a politician or a religious believer—opens the door to tragedy. All scientific information is imperfect, and we have to treat it with humility. Such, for him, was the human condition.

The imperfection of knowledge is also, crucially, a moral lesson. It is the lesson of twentieth-century painting from Cubism onward, but also that of quantum physics. All we can do is to push deeper and deeper into better approximations of an ever-evasive reality. The goal of complete understanding recedes as we approach it.

There is no God's-eye view, Dr. Bronowski insisted, and the people who claim that there is and that they possess it are not just wrong but morally pernicious. Errors are inextricably bound up with the pursuit of human knowledge, which requires more than mathematical calculation. It also requires insight, interpretation and a personal act of judgment for which we are *responsible*. The emphasis on the moral responsibility of knowledge was essential for all of Dr. Bronowski's work. The acquisition of knowledge entails a responsibility for the integrity of what we are as ethical creatures.

Dr. Bronowski's eleventh essay took him to the ancient university city of Göttingen, Germany, to explain the genesis of Werner Heisenberg's uncertainty principle in the hugely creative milieu that surrounded the physicist Max Born in the 1920s. Dr. Bronowski insisted that the principle of uncertainty was a misnomer because it gives the impression that in science (and outside it) we are always uncertain. But this is wrong. Knowledge is precise, but that precision is confined within a certain *toleration* of uncertainty. Heisenberg's insight was that the electron is a particle that yields only limited information; its speed and position are confined by the tolerance of Max Planck's quantum, the basic element of matter.

Dr. Bronowski thought that the uncertainty principle should therefore be called the principle of tolerance. Pursuing knowledge means accepting uncertainty. Heisenberg's principle has the consequence that no physical events can ultimately be described with absolute certainty, or with "zero tolerance," as it were. The more we know, the less certain we are.

In the everyday world, we accept a lack of ultimate exactitude with a melancholic shrug. Indeed, we constantly employ inexactitude in our relations with other people. Our relations also require a principle of tolerance. We encounter other people across a gray area of negotiation and approximation. Such is the business of listening and the back and forth of conversation and social interaction.

For Dr. Bronowski, the moral consequence of knowledge is that we must never judge others on the basis of some absolute, godlike conception of certainty. All knowledge, all information that passes between human beings, can be exchanged only within what he called "a play of tolerance," whether in science, literature, politics or religion. As Dr. Bronowski eloquently put it, "Human knowledge is personal and responsible, an unending adventure at the edge of uncertainty."

The relationships between humans and nature and between humans and other humans can take place only within a certain play of tolerance. Insisting on certainty, by contrast, leads ineluctably to arrogance and dogma based on ignorance.

At this point, in the final minutes of the show, the scene shifted to Auschwitz, where many members of Bronowski's family were murdered. Bronowski dipped his hand into the muddy water of a pond that contained the remains of his family members and the members of countless other families. All were victims of the same hatred: the hatred of the other. By contrast, he said—just before the camera hauntingly cut to slow motion—"We have to touch people." It was an extraordinary and moving moment.

The play of tolerance opposes the principle of monstrous certainty that is endemic to fascism and, sadly, not just to fascism but to all the various faces of fundamentalism. When we think we have certainty, when we aspire to the knowledge of the gods, Auschwitz can happen and can repeat itself. Arguably, it has repeated itself in the genocidal certainties of past decades.

The pursuit of scientific knowledge is as personal an act as lifting a paintbrush or writing a poem, and all those acts are profoundly human. If the human condition is defined by limitedness, that fact is glorious because moral limitedness is rooted in a faith in the power of the imagination, in our sense of responsibility and in our acceptance of our fallibility. We always have to acknowledge that we might be mistaken. When we forget that, we forget ourselves, and the worst can happen.

In 1945, nearly three decades before *The Ascent of Man*, Dr. Bronowski—who was a close friend of the Hungarian physicist Leo Szilard, the reluctant father of the atomic bomb— visited Nagasaki to help assess the damage wrought there by the second atomic bomb. What he saw convinced him to discontinue his research for the British military with which he had been engaged during the Second World War. From that time onward, he focused on the relations between science and human values. When someone said to Szilard in Bronowski's company that the bombing of Hiroshima and Nagasaki was science's tragedy, Szilard replied firmly that that was wrong: it was a human tragedy.

Such was Dr. Bronowski's lesson for a thirteen-year-old boy forty years ago. Being slightly old-school, I treated myself last Christmas to a DVD deluxe boxed set of *The Ascent of Man*. I am currently watching it with my ten-year-old stepson. Admittedly, it is not really much competition for Candy Crush, Minecraft and his sundry other screen obsessions, but he is showing an interest. Or at least he is tolerating my enthusiasm. And, of course, beginning to learn toleration is the whole point.

30

Nothing Remains
David Bowie's Vision of Love

January 11, 2016

On the title track of *Blackstar,* the David Bowie album released just a couple of days before his death on January 10, Bowie sings, "I'm not a pop star." True, he was an attractive celebrity with hit records, great hair and a gender-bending past. But for me, and for his millions of fans, he was someone who made life less ordinary. Indeed, Bowie's music made me feel alive for the first time. And if that sounds like overstatement, perhaps you don't get what music is about and what it can do.

For the hundreds of thousands of ordinary working-class boys and girls in England in the early 1970s, including me, Bowie incarnated something glamorous, enticing, exciting and mysterious: a world of unknown pleasures and sparkling intelligence. He offered an escape route from the suburban hellholes that we inhabited. Bowie spoke most eloquently to the disaffected, to those who didn't feel right in their skin, the socially awkward, the alienated. He spoke to the weirdos, the freaks, the outsiders, and drew us in to an extraordinary intimacy, although we knew the intimacy was total fantasy. But make no mistake, it was a love story. A love story that, in my case, has lasted forty-four years so far.

Now I'm hearing him sing "Nothing remains"—the opening words of "Sunday," the languid first track on the 2002 album *Heathen*. The song seems now like a lamentation, a prayer or a psalm for the dead. It is tempting to interpret these words in the light of Bowie's death, to believe that nothing remains for us after his death, that all is lost.

This interpretation would be a mistake.

The word "nothing" peppers and punctuates Bowie's entire body of work, from the "hold on to nothing" of "After All," from *The Man Who Sold the World*, through the scintillating, dystopian visions of *Diamond Dogs* and the refrain "We're nothing and nothing can help us," from *Heroes*, and onward all the way to *Blackstar*. One could base an entire coherent interpretation of Bowie's work by focusing on that one word, "nothing," and tracking its valences through his songs. Nothing is everywhere in Bowie.

Does that mean that Bowie was some sort of nihilist? Does it mean that his music, from the cultural disintegration of *Diamond Dogs*, through the depressive languor of *Low*, on to the apparent melancholia of "Lazarus," is a message of gloom and doom?

On the contrary.

Let's take *Blackstar*, the album that Bowie reportedly planned as a message to his fans from beyond the grave, which I and so many others have been listening to compulsively over the past few days. In the final track, "I Can't Give Everything Away," whose title is a response to the demand for meaning that Bowie's listeners kept making over the decades, he sings,

> Seeing more and feeling less
> Saying no but meaning yes

This is all I ever meant
That's the message that I sent

Within Bowie's negativity, beneath his apparent naysaying and gloom, one can hear a clear yes, an absolute and unconditional affirmation of life in all its chaotic complexity as well as its moments of transport and delight. For Bowie, I think, it is only when we clear away all the fakery of social convention, the popery and jiggery-pokery of organized religion, and the compulsory happiness that plague our culture that we can hear the yes that resounds across his music.

At the core of Bowie's music and his apparent negativity is a profound yearning for connection and, most of all, for love.

What was being negated by Bowie was all the nonsense, the falsity, the accrued social meanings, traditions and morass of identity that shackled us, especially in relation to gender identity and class. His songs revealed how fragile all these meanings are and gave us the capacity for reinvention. They gave us the belief that our capacity for change was, like his, seemingly limitless.

There are limits, obviously mortal limits, to who we are and how far we can reshape ourselves—even for Bowie, who seemed eternal. But when I listen to Bowie's songs, I hear an extraordinary hope for transformation. I don't think I am alone in this.

The core of this hope, which gives it a visceral register that touches the deepest level of our desire, is the sense that, as he sings in "Rock and Roll Suicide," "Oh no, love, you're not alone," the sense that we can be heroes, just for a day, and that we can be *us* just for a day, with some new sense of what it means to be us.

This hope also has a political meaning. Bowie was often wrongly seen, particularly back in the 1970s, as some kind of right-wing nationalist (I note, with some pleasure, that Bowie, unlike Mick Jagger and Paul McCartney, turned down the offer of a knighthood from the queen in 2003). There's another line from *Blackstar* that is particularly powerful. Bowie sings,

> If I'll never see the English evergreens I'm running to
> It's nothing to me
> It's nothing to see

Bowie will now never see those evergreens. But he was not conveying wistful nostalgia, for they are nothing to him and nothing to see. Concealed in Bowie's often dystopian words is an appeal to utopia, to the possible transformation not just of who we are but of where we are. Bowie, for me, belongs to the best of a utopian aesthetic tradition that longs for a yes within the cramped, petty relentless no of Englishness. What his music expressed a yearning for and allowed us to imagine were new forms of being together, new intensities of desire and love in keener visions and sharper sounds.

31

PBS

April 13, 2013

Let me tell you an odd story in anticipation of summer, should it ever come. Last June, just as New York was turning back into its usual summer sweatbox, my friend Shirley called my ex-wife, Jamieson, and said she knew someone with a pool in New Jersey. They were away for the weekend, and it was fine if we swam there.

One hour later, we'd crossed the bridge and were heading up Route 9W, windows open, looking out over the Hudson River. It was a lovely day. I suggested that we stop for supplies, snacks and drinks. I was the last of the three of us to leave the gas station with a bag bulging with goodies.

I walked into a situation in the parking lot. Three cars, one of them Shirley's, were simultaneously trying to pull out of their parking spots. The two other drivers were screaming at each other, at Shirley and at Jamieson. Ever the conquering diplomatic hero, I decided to intervene. Channeling some bizarre amalgam of Basil Fawlty and Rodney King, the latter in his "Can't we all get along?" moment, I said, "Come on, gentleman, let's be reasonable. We can settle this amicably and all be on our way."

Big mistake. The first driver, in a black SUV, gave me the finger while accusing me of having had sex with my mother (which was, moreover, completely untrue) before making a wheel-spinning exit from the parking lot.

In a spirit of hopeful solidarity, I shrugged my shoulders and raised my eyebrows in disbelief at the actions of the first driver for the second driver's benefit. He was driving a red sports convertible. I turned and made my way back to Shirley's car.

That was when things really kicked off. The sports car guy screamed at me, also accusing me of having had sex with my mother (untrue) and dropping as well an impressive number of unprintable adjectival expletives that circled around my being bald (true) and speaking like a limey (undeniable).

I paused for a moment, wheeled around, straightened my back, and slowly walked toward the sports car, my carrier bag, full of diet sodas and trail mix, rustling in the soft breeze. I took a good long look at the guy. He was nicely, if casually, dressed, with expensive shades and a deeply impressive mop of black hair. It was thick and gleaming with some kind of styling product. I said, "Excuse me, sir. Would you perhaps like to apologize?"

Right then I realized my huge mistake. Back home, after Shirley called, I had quickly found my swimming trunks and earplugs, pulled on some jeans and flip-flops and buttoned up a newish shirt, a birthday gift.

Let me tell you about the shirt. I loved this shirt! It was a beautiful, brushed-cotton button-down in a dusty, slightly shocking pink. What's more, it had cost two hundred dollars. That's right, two hundred dollars! I wore it to please myself and my ex and, on this occasion, to impress Shirley, who is a CEO in the fashion industry.

Pride first; fall second. The sports car guy lowered his shades, looked at me in my pink shirt and yelled, "Who are you looking at, pudendum boy? Why are you wearing a pudendum boy shirt, pudendum boy?" (I should point out that the sports car guy did not use the Latin term but another noun beginning with "p," which both my own pusillanimousness and the impeccable manners of this newspaper forbid naming.)

I was somewhat taken aback. I mean, this was a nice shirt, right? This was a two-hundred-dollar shirt. This was a goddamn Steven Alan shirt. Maybe it was the color of Pepto-Bismol. Maybe I looked a little like living diarrhea relief. But this was no pudendum boy shirt. I live in Brooklyn. I keep it real.

Warming to his theme and realizing he had the upper hand, the sports car guy began to improvise, Coltrane-style, on his theme. Again, the number and rapidity of obscenities was impressive, but if I could summarize the drift of his reasoning it would be as follows:

1. By virtue of the fact that I was wearing what we can call for the sake of economy a PBS, and,
2. On the basis of the assumption, once again repeated (but still untrue), of my having had sex with my mother,
3. He was inviting me to perform fellatio on him.

He emphasized the invitation with explicit hand gestures and pointed repeatedly to the area of his crotch. I am not that slow. I got the point. And so it went round and round for ages like a three-stroke engine: PBS, incest, fellatio.

I was impressed by this bravura display of American masculinity. But I was also bewildered by it. What exactly was he asking me to do to him? Wasn't there dissonance between my alleged capacity for incest and the effeminate connotations of the PBS? Was it the pinkness of the shirt that led to the insinuation that I should fellate the sports car guy? And—most of all—who was the PB in this situation? Me or him? Surely him, I thought. He was apparently initiating some kind of homosexual liaison between us. I was just buying soda and trail mix.

My head spinning, I fell silent. He slipped his shift into drive and the car purred into motion. As he left the parking lot I screamed, "Learn some manners!" I don't think he heard me. I tramped back to the car where Jamieson and Shirley were laughing uncontrollably, tears in their eyes. "That went quite well," I said with some pride. "At least I didn't swear back or rise to his obscene bait. I was clearly occupying the moral high ground."

The rest of the day passed off peacefully enough. Frankly, the pool was disappointingly small. Undressing that night, I looked hard at my pink shirt as I put it back on the hanger. I gazed at it quizzically for the longest time. Maybe the sports car guy had a point? "Don't be so bloody stupid," I said to myself.

But I never wore the shirt again.

It lies folded in a drawer. I'm looking at it right now. All I can think when I see it is "PBS! PBS! PBS!" It's as if the shirt is screaming obscenities at me in a Jersey accent. I close the drawer.

After a couple of glasses of wine, I have once or twice tried to tell some version of this story at parties because I don't know what it means. New York guys usually reply by saying (again, I paraphrase, for the sake of decency), "Why didn't you tell him to engage in a sexual act with himself?" "What do you mean?" I reply. "Should I respond to his request for fellatio with me by suggesting that he have sex with himself, should such an act be physically possible? He didn't look like the kind of chap that did extreme yoga."

So what is the moral of this little tale? Don't wear pink shirts in the summer in New Jersey? Hardly. Is it about nobly intended moral interventions often having bizarre consequences? We've known that for quite some time. Sophocles had some thoughts on the matter.

It's more about the way words can wound in the oddest ways. Even though the currency of swearwords has become dramatically devalued through overcirculation, they still harbor a power of transgressive pleasure and can inflict pain. As people in my line of work are wont to say, we could do with a richer phenomenology of swearing.

We know swearwords are literally meaningless (he didn't mean for me to perform fellatio on him. I would not have meant for him to have sex with himself, etc., etc., etc.), yet they carry a force that compels us. This is why many of us like to swear a lot. It feels good to swear and bad to be sworn at. Swearing always aims at something really intimate, something usually hidden, which is why the words are so explicitly and violently sexual. But in hurting us they can hit the bull's-eye, or balls-eye, of an unpleasant truth that we'd rather not accept.

So the sports car guy was right. I am that smug, self-righteous fool who lives in a fashionable corner of Brooklyn with the two-hundred-dollar Steven Alan shirt, going to a private swimming pool in my friend's car with my little bag of snacks to escape the city heat. It's pathetic. That pink shirt is a PBS, and I am a PB. I deserved what I got.

I've made a resolution. This summer I'm going to take my PBS out of the drawer, wash it, and wear it with pride. If you see me sporting it in the street, in a car, or in a gas station parking lot, be sure to yell out some pudendal obscenity. Thank you in advance from the bottom of my heart for all your future abuse.

Philip K. Dick, Garage
Philosopher

32

Meditations on a Radiant Fish

May 20, 2012

When I believe, I am crazy.
When I don't believe, I suffer psychotic depression.

—Philip K. Dick

Philip K. Dick is arguably the most influential writer of science fiction in the past half-century. In his short and meteoric career, he wrote 121 short stories and 45 novels. His work was successful during his lifetime but has grown exponentially in influence since his death in 1982. Dick's work will probably be best known through the dizzyingly successful Hollywood adaptations of his work, in movies like *Blade Runner* (based on "Do Androids Dream of Electric Sheep?"), *Total Recall*, *Minority Report*, *A Scanner Darkly* and, most recently, *The Adjustment Bureau*. Yet few people might consider Dick a thinker. This would be a mistake.

Dick's life has long passed into legend, sprinkled with florid tales of madness and intoxication. Some consider the legend a diversion from the character of Dick's literary brilliance. Jonathan Lethem writes—rightly in my view—"Dick wasn't a

legend and he wasn't mad. He lived among us and was a genius."
Yet Dick's life continues to obtrude massively into any assessment of his work.

Everything turns here on an event that Dickheads refer to with the catchphrase "the golden fish." On February 20, 1974, Dick was hit with the force of an extraordinary revelation after a visit to the dentist for an impacted wisdom tooth, for which he had received a dose of sodium pentothal. A young woman delivered a bottle of Darvon tablets to his apartment in Fullerton, California. She was wearing a necklace with the pendant of a golden fish, an ancient Christian symbol that had been adopted by the Jesus counterculture movement of the late 1960s.

The fish pendant, on Dick's account, began to emit a golden ray of light, and Dick suddenly experienced what he called, with a nod to Plato, anamnesis: the recollection or total recall of the entire sum of knowledge. Dick claimed to have access to what philosophers call intellectual intuition: the direct perception by the mind of a metaphysical reality behind screens of appearance. Many philosophers since Kant have insisted that intellectual intuition is available to human beings only in the guise of fraudulent obscurantism, usually as religious or mystical experience, like Emanuel Swedenborg's visions of the angelic multitude. This is what Kant called, in a lovely German word, *die Schwärmerei*, a kind of swarming enthusiasm, where the self is literally enthused with God, *o theos*. Brusquely sweeping aside the limitations and strictures that Kant placed on the different domains of pure and practical reason, the phenomenal and the noumenal, Dick claimed direct intuition of the ultimate nature of what he called "true reality."

The golden fish episode was just the beginning. In the following days and weeks, Dick experienced and indeed enjoyed night-long psychedelic visions with phantasmagoric light shows. Such hypnagogic episodes continued off and on, together with hearing voices and having prophetic dreams, until his death eight years later at age fifty-three. Many very weird things happened—too many to list here—including incidents with a clay pot that Dick called Ho On (which is close to the ancient Greek word for "being") or "Oh Ho," which spoke to him about various deep spiritual issues in a brash and irritable voice.

Now, was bad acid the explanation, or was good sodium pentothal? Or was Dick seriously bonkers? Was he psychotic? Was he schizophrenic? (He writes, "The schizophrenic is a leap ahead that failed.") Were the visions the effect of a series of brain seizures that some call TLE—temporal lobe epilepsy? Could we now explain and explain away Dick's revelatory experiences by some better neuroscientific story about the brain? Perhaps. But the problem is that each of these causal explanations misses the richness of the phenomena that Dick was trying to describe and also overlooks his unique means for describing them.

After Dick experienced the events of what he came to call 2–3-74 (the events of February and March of that year), he devoted the rest of his life to trying to understand what had happened to him. For Dick, understanding meant writing. Suffering from what we might call chronic hypergraphia, between 2–3-74 and his death Dick wrote more than eight thousand pages about his experience. He often wrote all night, producing twenty single-spaced narrow-margined pages at a go; they were largely handwritten and littered with extraordinary diagrams and cryptic sketches.

The unfinished mountain of paper, assembled posthumously into ninety-one folders, was called "Exegesis." The fragments were assembled by Dick's friend Paul Williams and then sat in his garage in Glen Ellen, California, for the several years. A beautifully edited selection of these texts, with a golden fish on the cover, was finally published at the end of 2011, a mighty 950-page tome. It represents just a fraction of the whole.

Dick writes, "My exegesis, then, is an attempt to understand my own understanding." The book is the most extraordinary and extended act of self-interpretation, a seemingly endless thinking on the events of 2–3-74 that always seems to begin anew. Often dull, repetitive and given over to expressions of massive paranoia, *Exegesis* also possesses many passages of genuine brilliance and is marked by an utter and utterly disarming sincerity. At times, as in the epigraph above, Dick falls into dejection and despair. At other moments, like some latter-day Simon Magus, he is possessed of a manic swelling-up of the ego to unify with the divine: "I was in the mind of God."

To understand what happened to him on 2–3-74, Dick used the resources that he had at hand and that he liked best. These were a complete set of the fifteenth edition of the *Encyclopaedia Britannica* that Dick purchased late in 1974 and Paul Edwards's arguably unsurpassed *Encyclopedia of Philosophy*, published in eight handsome volumes in 1967, one of the richest and most capacious philosophical documents ever produced. Dick's reading was haphazard and eclectic. Encyclopedias permitted an admittedly untutored rapidity of association that lent a certain formal and systematic coherence to his wide-ranging obsessions.

Skimming through and across multiple encyclopedia entries, Dick found links and correspondences of ideas everywhere. He also stumbled into the primary texts of a number of philosophers and theologians—notably the pre-Socratics, Plato, Meister Eckhart, Spinoza, Hegel, Schopenhauer, Marx, Whitehead, Heidegger and Hans Jonas. His interpretations are sometimes bizarre but often compelling.

This leads me to an important point. Dick was a consummate autodidact. He survived for less than one semester at college, at the University of California, Berkeley, in 1949, taking and quitting Philosophy 10A in the space of a few weeks. Dick left the class in disgust at the ignorance and intolerance of his instructor when he asked his professor about the plausibility of Plato's metaphysical theory of the forms—the truth of which was later proven for Dick by the experience of 2-3-74. Dick was evidently not trained as a philosopher or theologian—although I abhor that verb "trained," which makes academics sound like domestic pets. Dick was an amateur philosopher, or, to borrow a phrase from one of the editors of *Exegesis,* Erik Davis, he was that most splendid of things: a garage philosopher.

What Dick lacks in academic and scholarly rigor, he more than makes up for in powers of imagination and rich lateral, cumulative association. If he had known more, he might have produced less interesting chains of ideas. In a later remark in *Exegesis,* Dick writes, "I am a fictionalizing philosopher, not a novelist." He interestingly goes on to add, "The core of my writing is not art but truth." We seem to be facing an apparent paradox, where the concern with truth, the classical goal of the philosopher, is not judged to be in opposition to fiction but is itself a work a fiction. Dick saw his fiction writing as the creative attempt to describe what he discerned as the true reality. "I am basically analytical, not creative," he declared. "My writing is simply a creative way of handling analysis."

33

Future Gnostic

In the previous post, we looked at the consequences and possible philosophic import of the events of February and March of 1974 (also known as 2–3-74) in the life and work of Philip K. Dick, a period in which a dose of sodium pentothal, a light-emitting fish pendant and decades of fiction writing and quasi-philosophic activity came together in a revelation that led to Dick's eight-thousand-page "Exegesis." An edition was published in 2011.

May 21, 2012

So, what is the nature of the true reality that Dick claims to have intuited during the psychedelic visions of 2–3-74? Does his description unwind into mere structureless ranting and raving, or does it suggest some tradition of thought or belief? I would argue the latter. This is where things admittedly get a little weirder in an already weird universe, so hold on tight.

In the very first lines of *Exegesis* Dick writes, "We see the Logos addressing the many living entities." Logos is an important concept that litters the pages of *Exegesis*. It is a word with a wide variety of meanings in ancient Greek, one of which is indeed "word." It can also mean "speech, reason" (in Latin, *ratio*) or giving an account of something. For Heraclitus, to whom Dick frequently refers, logos is the universal law that governs the cosmos, of which most human beings are somnolently ignorant. Dick certainly has this latter meaning in mind, but—most important—logos refers to the opening of John's Gospel, "In the beginning was the word" (*logos*), where the word becomes flesh in the person of Christ.

But the core of Dick's vision is not quite Christian in the traditional sense. It is gnostical: it is mystical intellection, at its highest moment a fusion with a transmundane or alien God who is identified with logos and who can communicate with human beings in the form of a ray of light or, in Dick's case, hallucinatory visions.

There is a tension throughout *Exegesis* between a monistic view of the cosmos (where there is just one substance in the universe, which can be seen in Dick's references to Spinoza's idea of God as nature, Whitehead's idea of reality as process and Hegel's dialectic where "the true is the whole"), and a dualistic or gnostical view of the cosmos, with two cosmic forces in conflict, one malevolent and the other benevolent. The way I read Dick, the latter view wins out. This means that the visible, phenomenal world is fallen and indeed a kind of prison cell, cage or cave.

Christianity, lest it be forgotten, is a metaphysical monism that obliges every Christian to love every aspect of creation—even the foulest and smelliest—because it is the work of God. Evil is not substantial because if it were, it would have to have been caused by God, who is good by definition. Against this, Gnosticism declares a radical dualism between the false God, who created this world—who is usually called the demiurge—and the true God, who is unknown and alien to this world. For the Gnostic, evil is substantial, and its evidence is the world. There is a story of a radical Gnostic who used to wash himself in his own saliva in order to have as little contact as possible with creation. Gnosticism is the worship of an alien God by those alienated from the world.

The novelty of Dick's Gnosticism is that the divine is alleged to communicate with us through information. This is a persistent theme in Dick, and he refers to the universe as information and even Christ as information. Such information has a kind of electrostatic life connected to the theory of what he calls orthogonal time. This rich and strange idea of time is completely at odds with the standard, linear conception, which goes back to Aristotle. In the standard conception, time is a sequence of now-points extending from the future through the present and into the past. Both ends of the timeline disappear into infinity. Dick explains orthogonal time as a circle that contains everything. In an arresting image, he claims that orthogonal time contains "everything which was, just as grooves on an LP contain that part of the music which has already been played; they don't disappear after the stylus tracks them."

His time is like that seemingly endless final chord in the Beatles' "A Day in the Life" that gathers more and more momentum and musical complexity as it decays. In other words, orthogonal time permits total recall.

In his wilder moments—and, to be honest, they occur often—Dick declares that orthogonal time will make it possible for the return of the golden age, namely the time before the Fall and prior to original sin. He also claims that in orthogonal time the future falls back into and fulfills itself in the present. This is doubtless why Dick believed that his fiction was becoming truth, that the future was unfolding in his books. If we think for a second about how the technologies of security in the contemporary world seem to resemble the 2055 of *Minority Report* more and more each day, it seems that maybe Dick has a point. Maybe he was writing the future.

Toward the end of *Exegesis,* Dick begins to borrow and quote liberally from *The Gnostic Religion* by Hans Jonas, a wonderful book that first appeared in English in 1958. It is not difficult to see why Jonas's book spoke to Dick somewhat like the aforementioned clay pot. Jonas shows the force and persistence—both historical and conceptual—of the idea of enlightenment by the ray of divine light, the mystical *gnosis theou* (knowledge of God, a Gnostic doctrine), the direct beholding of the divine reality. The core of Gnosticism is this direct contact with the divine, which itself divinizes the soul and allows it to see the vile world for what it is: nothing. At the core of Gnosticism, for Jonas, is an experience of nihilism, namely that the phenomenal world is nothing and the true world is nothing to be seen phenomenally but requires the divine illumination to be seen. Divine illumination is reserved for the few, for the secretive elect.

Dick's *Exegesis* is a peculiarly powerful and poignant restatement of a gnostical worldview. Right or wrong—and, to be clear, I am not a Gnostic—Gnosticism still represents, in my view, a powerful temptation that needs to be understood before being criticized. Dick writes, and one can find passages like this all over *Exegesis:*

> So there is a secret within a secret. The Empire is a secret (its existence and its power; that it rules) and secondly the secret illegal Christians pitted against it. So the discovery of the secret illegal Christians instantly causes one to grasp that, if they exist illegally, something evil that is stronger is in power, right here!

This is a succinct and revealing statement of the politics of Dick's Gnosticism. The logic here is close to that put forth by various

Gnostic sects of the early Christian period, like the Valentinians and the Manicheans, through to the Cathars and the much-feared "Heresy of the Free Spirit" that some historians have claimed was like an invisible empire across Europe in the thirteenth and fourteenth centuries.

The core of the heresy consists in the denial of original sin: sin does not lie within us but within the world, which is not the creation of the true God but of the malevolent demiurge, whom Saint Paul calls in one quasi-gnostical moment "the God of this world." Therefore, we must see through the evil illusion of this world to the true world of the alien God. The phenomenal world is the creation of a bad God and governed over by those agents of the demiurge that the Gnostics called the archons, the rulers or governors, and that Dick lumps together as the Empire.

When we learn to identify the true worldly source of sin, the Gnostics instruct, we can begin the process of unifying with the divine by divorcing ourselves from the phenomenal world. At the end of this process, we become divine ourselves and can throw off the rule of the evil empire that governs the world. This link between mystical experience and political insurgency is suggested throughout *Exegesis*. We are slaves to the Empire, in other words, and the world is a prison from which we need to free ourselves. The Gnostics called it "the puny cell of the creator God." Dick calls it the BIP, the Black Iron Prison, which is opposed to the spiritual redemption offered in the PTG, the Palm Tree Garden.

Note the emphasis on secrecy. The first secret is that the world is governed by malevolent imperial or governmental elites that together form a kind of a covert coven. The world itself is a college of corporations linked together by money and serving only the interests of the business leaders and shareholders. The second secret—"a secret within a secret"—belongs to those few who have swallowed the red pill, torn through the veil of Maya, contacted the divine. In other words, they have seen the "matrix"—a pop culture allusion that may lead us to some surprising, even alarming, contemporary implications of the gnostical worldview, as explicated in the next essay.

34
Adventures in the Dream Factory

May 22, 2012

In the previous post, we looked at Philip K. Dick's intellectual and philosophical ties to the early Gnostics. Now, culturally and politically at least, it's time to look at the Gnostics in the mirror.

Philip K. Dick's admittedly peculiar but passionately held worldview and the Gnosticism it encapsulates does more than explain what some call the dystopian turn in science fiction from the 1960s onward. It also gives us what has arguably become the dominant mode of understanding of fiction in our time, whether literary, artistic or cinematic. This is the idea that reality is a pernicious illusion, a repressive and authoritarian matrix generated in a dream factory that we need to tear down in order to see things aright and have access to the truth. And let's be honest: it is immensely pleasurable to give oneself over to the idea that one has torn aside the veil of illusion and seen the truth—"I am one of the elect, one of the few in the know, in the *gnosis*."

Dick's Gnosticism also allows us to see in a new light what is existentially the toughest teaching of traditional Christianity:

that sin lies within us in the form of original sin. Once we embrace Gnosticism, we can declare that wickedness does not have its source within the human heart but out there, with the corrupt archons of corporate capitalism or whomever. We are not wicked. It is the world that is wicked. This insight finds its modern voice in Rousseau before influencing a Heinz variety of Romanticisms that turn on the idea of natural human goodness and childhood innocence. We adults idealize childhood because grown-up life seems such a disaster. We forget that being a child—being that powerless—is often its very own disaster.

On the gnostical view, once we see the wicked world for what it is, we can step back and rediscover our essential goodness, the divine spark within us, our purity, our authenticity. It is this very desire for purity and authenticity that drives the whole wretched industry of New Age obscurantism and its multiple techniques of spiritual and material detox, its quasi-cultic multimillion-dollar-grossing insistence on the Secret. Against this toxic view of the world, I think we need to emphasize what splendidly impure and inauthentic creatures we are. Whatever spark is within us is not divine but all too human.

Aside from *The Matrix* trilogy and the direct movie adaptations of Dick's fiction, two recent movies have strong gnostical themes: those of the Danish film writer and director Lars von Trier. For our purposes here, they may be described in a few brief lines.

In *Antichrist* (2009), the character played by Charlotte Gainsbourg says, "Nature is Satan's church"; in *Melancholia* (2011), the Kirsten Dunst character says to the Charlotte Gainsbourg character, "All I know is that life on earth is evil." What is not gnostical in Von Trier is the supplementary insistence that if life is evil, then there is no life elsewhere. We should welcome the collision of the rogue planet Melancholia with the earth precisely for this reason: to bring an end to evil.

A purer version of the gnostical ideology of authenticity can found in the biggest grossing movie of all time in America, James Cameron's 2009 epic, *Avatar*. By 2154, earth's resources have been used up and its surface reduced to a filthy, poisoned husk. The corrupt and all-powerful RDA Corporation is mining for the appropriately named Unobtainium on the planet Pandora. This planet is home to the Na'vi—blue-skinned, beautiful, ten-foot-tall beings—who have an intimate connection with nature and who worship the mother goddess, Eywa. Jake, the broken, disabled ex-Marine, eventually becomes his alien Na'vi avatar, melds with his true love Naytiri, and unifies with nature after defeating the satanic human forces of corporate evil. He loses his human identity and becomes the alien, leaving behind him the poisoned, destroyed homeland of earth for the blessed alien land. The point is that authentic harmony with nature can be achieved only by throwing off the garment of earthly nature and becoming alien. Such is the basic fantasy of Gnosticism.

Dick's Gnosticism enables us to understand something of the paranoid style of American politics—and perhaps not just American politics. For example, Dick constantly comes back to the theme of Watergate and the rather odd idea that the removal of President Nixon was the reassertion of the true deity over the false idols of the cave. He thinks, in other words, that the phenomenal world is a prison governed by corrupt, secretive and malevolent elites. There are too many political analogues to this view to list here. Think, for example, about the relentless rise of conspiracy theories, which has gone hand in hand with the vast, rhizomatic flourishing of the internet. Think about the widespread idea—on the right and the left—that the United States is governed by secretive, all-powerful elites. These used to be identified as Ivy League–educated WASPs or Freemasons or Jews and are now usually identified as former senior employees of Goldman Sachs.

If you think that "they" are hiding a secret from the rest of us and that learning it requires the formation of a small, secret sect to work against them, you have entered into an essentially gnostical way of thinking. Politics here becomes the defense of purity against impure, inauthentic forces, and the true leader has to be an authentic hero who can combat the forces of evil with an almost superhuman resolve.

The morality of Gnosticism is oddly relevant to our current situation. As Hans Jonas points out, possessors of *gnosis* set themselves apart from the great, soiled mass of humankind. Hatred of the world was also a contempt for worldly morality, for which there were two equal, but opposed, ethical responses: asceticism and libertinage.

The ascetic infers from access to gnosis that the world is a toxic, contaminating machine with which one should have as little contact as possible. This argument can be seen as consistent with contemporary culture and the cult of detox, which insists on purifying the body and soul against environmental, nutritional and sexual contact in order to find and safeguard the divine spark within. The awful truth of contemporary asceticism is powerfully played out in another film, Todd Haynes's brilliant *Safe* (1995), in which the character played by Julianne Moore develops a total allergy to life. Her so-called environmental illness leads her eventually to a self-help cult in the California desert, where she lives alone in a hypoallergenic pod muttering to her image in the mirror, "I love myself" and other mantras.

The flip side of the ascetic is the libertine: the person whose access to gnosis implies both absolute freedom and absolute protection. One thinks of the "Do what thou wilt!" hermetic charlatanism of Aleister Crowley. But one also thinks—I have heard this story on countless occasions, often late at night—of the New York urban myth of the hugely wealthy finance guy who deliberately wanders drunk or stoned into oncoming traffic. He knows that he will be safe from harm. Because fate is on his side, he is therefore free to do whatever he wills. Once you have access to the Secret, the forces of the universe align with your desires.

In the face of an alienating and poisonous world, one can either withdraw to a safe, allergic distance or plunge headlong into the viral whirlpool of humanity. Either way, the libertine expects to be okay.

Crazy as it doubtless must sound, Dick's Gnosticism responds, I think, to a deep and essential anxiety of our late modern times. The irrepressible rise of a deterministic scientific worldview threatens to invade and overtake all those areas of human activity that we associate with literature, culture, history, religion, and the rest.

Ask yourself: What does one do in the face of a monistic all-consuming naturalism? We can embrace it, hoping to wrest whatever shards of wonder and meaning we can from inquiries into the brain or the cosmos sold as brightly colored trade hardbacks, written by reputable, often prize-winning scientists. Or we can reject scientific determinism by falling back into some version of dualism. That could mean embracing a spiritual or religious metaphysics of whatever confection or—if one is still nostalgic for the disappointed modernism of, say, Kafka or Beckett—it could mean accepting the life of a lonely, alienated self in a heartless world of anomie.

But perhaps another way is open, one that is neither entirely naturalistic nor religious, nor some redux of modernist miserabilism. If so, to quote Jonas, "philosophy must find it out." Such is the path that I have tried to tread in the essays in this book.

Covid Coda

35

Our Fear, Our Trembling, Our Strength

April 10, 2020

We're scared. We're on edge. We're unable to concentrate. We can't find focus. Our minds hop around flealike from one update to the next. We follow the news, because we feel we should. And then we wish we hadn't, because it's terrifying and sad. Daytime naps seem involuntary and fitful. Sleep will often not descend. When it does, we sometimes wake in a mortal panic, with hypochondriac symptoms we feel to be real but we know are not; and then we feel selfishly stupid for having them in the first place. We take our temperature. We wait. We take it again. It goes on. Feelings of powerlessness and ennui slide into impotent rage at what is being done and, most of all, what is not being done, or is being done poorly, irresponsibly, dishonestly.

The thought of dying alone with a respiratory sickness is horrifying. The knowledge that this is what is happening to thousands of people right here, right now, is unbearable. Lives are being lost and livelihoods ravaged. Metaphors of war feel worn out and fraudulent. The social structures, habits and ways of life we took for granted are dissolving. Other people are possible sources of contagion, and so are we. We advance masked and keep our distance.

Each of us is adrift on our own ghost ship. It is so eerily quiet here in New York City. Comical memes circulate. We feel a moment's mirth, share with our friends, and slide back into separateness, teeth clenched. A few weeks into this new situation, the initial fever of communication and the novelty of long phone calls with close or distant friends had subsided into something more somber, more sullen and altogether more serious. We know we're in it for the long haul, whatever that might mean.

How can we, or how should we, cope?

Philosophers have had a long, tortured love affair with social distancing, beginning with Socrates confined to his cell. René Descartes withdrew from the horrors of the Thirty Years' War (in which he was a participant) into a room in the Netherlands to ponder the nature of certainty. Others, like Boethius, Thomas More and Antonio Gramsci, are part of this long tradition of isolation and thought.

But what of philosophy itself? It has long been derided for its practical uselessness, its three-thousand-year track record of failing to solve humankind's most profound problems. How might it help us through this immensely difficult moment? Can philosophy offer illumination, even consolation, in this devastated new reality marked by anxiety, grief and the specter of death?

Perhaps this: To philosophize is to learn how to die. This is how Michel de Montaigne, the sixteenth-century French essayist, inventor of the genre of the essay, puts it, quoting Cicero, who was himself thinking of Socrates condemned to death. Montaigne says that he developed the habit of having death not just in his imagination but constantly in his mouth—in the food he ate and the drink he imbibed. For those of you who have taken up cooking and are perhaps drinking a little too much in your isolation, this might sound morbid. Not at all. Montaigne completes this thought with this astonishing sentence: "He who has learned how to die has unlearned how to be a slave." What an amazing idea: that slavery consists in bondage to the fear of death, that it is the terror of annihilation that keeps us enslaved.

Liberty, by contrast, consists in accepting our mortality, accepting that we are bound to die. Freedom is felt truly only in the knowledge that our lives are shaped by death's inevitable and ineluctable approach, day by day, hour by hour. In this view, a life lived well, a philosophical life, is one that welcomes death's approach. Existence is finite. Death is certain. This is hardly news. But a philosophical life has to begin from an impassioned affirmation of our finitude. As T. S. Eliot said of the Jacobean playwright John Webster, we have to see the skull beneath the skin.

Yet we're still scared. We're still on edge. Let's try and think about this in terms of a distinction between fear and anxiety. We've known at least since Aristotle that fear is our reaction to an actual threat in the world. Imagine that I have a strong fear of bears. If a huge bear showed up at the door of my apartment, I would feel terror (and quite possibly surprise). And if the bear retreated into the street, my fear would evaporate.

Anxiety, by contrast, has no particular object, no bear. It is instead a state in which the particular facts of the world recede from view. Everything feels uncanny and strange. It is a feeling of being in the world as a whole, a feeling about everything and nothing in particular. I would argue that what many of us are feeling right now is this profound anxiety.

The peculiar nature of the pandemic is that the virus is, while all too real, invisible to the naked eye and all pervasive. Covid-19 has formed itself into the structure of reality: a disease everywhere and nowhere, imprecisely known and, as yet, untreatable. Most of us have the feeling of having been swimming in a sea of virus for many months. But perhaps beneath the trembling of fear lies a deeper anxiety, the anxiety of being mortal, the anxiety of being pulled toward death. This is what we might try to seize hold of as a condition of our freedom.

It is vitally important, I think, to accept and affirm anxiety and not hide away from it or flee or evade it, or seek to explain it in relation to some object or cause. Our anxiety is not a disorder that needs medicated into numbness. It needs to be acknowledged, shaped and honed into a vehicle of liberation. I'm not saying that doing this is easy. But we can try to transform the basic mood of anxiety from something crippling into something enabling.

Most of us, most of the time, are encouraged by what passes as normality to live in a counterfeit eternity. We imagine that life will go on and that death happens to others. Death is reduced to what Heidegger calls a social inconvenience or downright tactlessness. The consolation of philosophy in this instance consists in pulling away from the death-denying habits of normal life and facing the anxiety of the situation with a clear-eyed courage and sober realism. Passionately rejecting those habits, accepting realism and enacting courage can be a basis for a shared response. Finitude is relational, not a question of just my death but the deaths of others, those we care about, near and far, friends and strangers.

A few weeks ago I found myself talking blithely about plague literature: Boccaccio's *Decameron*, Defoe's *A Journal of the Plague Year*, Camus's *The Plague*. I thought I was clever until I realized a lot of other people were saying the exact same things. In truth, the thinker I have been most deeply drawn back to is the brilliant seventeenth-century French mathematician and theologian Blaise Pascal, in particular his *Pensées*.

Pascal writes that the inability to sit quietly alone in a room is the source of all humanity's problems: of inconstancy, boredom and anxiety as defining traits of the human condition; of the machinelike power of habit and the gnawing noise of human pride. But most of all, it is Pascal's thought that the human being is a reed, "the weakest of nature," that each of us can be wiped away by a vapor—or an airborne droplet—that grips me.

Human beings are wretched, Pascal reminds us. We are weak, fragile, vulnerable, dependent creatures. But—and this is the vital twist—our wretchedness is our greatness. The universe can crush us, a virus can destroy us. But the universe knows none of this, and the virus does not care. We, by contrast, know that we are mortal. Our dignity consists in this thought. "Let us strive," Pascal says, "to think well. That is the principle of morality." I see this emphasis on human fragility, weakness, vulnerability, dependence and wretchedness as the opposite of morbidity and any fatuous pessimism. It is the key to our greatness. Our weakness is our strength.

Index

theater: ancient Athenian
democracy and, 143–45; fiction
as vehicle for presenting truth
in, 104; political role of, 144; as
recurring theme, 114; sports
stadiums in relation to theaters,
117–18. *See also* Athens;
memory theaters; tragedies
Thebes, 98, 135
Theophrastus, 136, 138
Thrasymachus, 78
Thucydides: *The History of the
Peloponnesian War*, 22–24
time: orthogonal time, 214;
pettifogger's time to speak in
court, 70–71, 77; philosopher's
limitless amount of, 71, 77
"To be or not to be" soliloquy
(*Hamlet*), 103–6
tolerance, principle of, 192–93
topos (association of memory with
place), 123
Total Recall (film), 207
The Towers of Lebanon (documentary), 109
tragedies: chorus and, 141;
competition in Athenian theater,
141–42; Greek history and,
114–15; polyphony of, 145;
sponsorship of plays in ancient
Greece, 141–42; Theater of
Dionysus as first place for
enactment of, 143; what
constitutes, 97–99
Trinity, 33
Triptolemos, 152
Trojan War, 115
Trump, Donald, 90, 92–93, 114
trust: money and, 56–57; Trump
creating distrust, 93
truth: Philip K. Dick claiming that
his science fiction is becoming

truth, 214; faith and, 41; news
cycle and, 92; theater's fiction as
vehicle for presenting, 104
tyranny and tyrants. *See* authoritarianism

uncertainty, 92; Heisenberg's
uncertainty principle, 192
undergraduate teachers, role of,
179–88. *See also* Cioffi, Frank
unemployment, 18
University of Essex, 181
utopia in David Bowie's lyrics, 198

Valentinians, 216
violence: art and music as conduit
to suspension of, 119–20;
constant presence in today's
world, 125; definition of,
112–13; in *Hamlet*, 101–7, 117;
justice understood as vengeance,
114; political, 113, 116; racial,
113, 119; revenge for 9/11
terrorist attacks, 108–11,
113–14; sports and, 117–19
Voltaire: *Candide*, 138
von Trier, Lars, 219

war on terror, 108–11, 113–14
water: meditation and, 8–9; time
and, 70, 77
Watergate, 220
Weber, Max, 185
Webster, Jamieson, 15, 101
Webster, John, 227
well-being as goal of human life,
15, 16
Wessel, David: *In Fed We Trust*, 57
Whitehead, Alfred North, 69, 210,
213
Whitman, Walt, 38; *Leaves of
Grass*, 5